BODYLINE

BODYLINE

PHILIP DERRIMAN

Foreword by Bill O'Reilly

COLLINS
THE SYDNEY MORNING HERALD

© Philip Derriman and John Fairfax 1984

First published 1984 by William Collins Pty Ltd, Sydney
Reprinted 1985
Typeset in Brisbane by Post Typesetters
Printed in Hong Kong

National Library of Australia
Cataloguing-in-Publication data

Derriman, Philip, 1943- .
Bodyline.

ISBN 0 00 216577 5

1. Cricket — Bowling — Pictorial works.
2. Cricket — Australia — History — Pictorial
works. 3. Cricket — England — History — Pictorial
works. I. Title.

796.35′822′0222

FOREWORD

It would be safe to say that Douglas Jardine was the one Englishman amongst all fifty millions of them who could have led the 1932–33 English touring team successfully throughout the whole test campaign using the tactics that had been decided upon beforehand for doing the job. Had the English selectors and the MCC, then the supreme cricket power, decided to stage an aptitude test instead of pedalling the captaincy job as they did, Jardine would have topped the list so convincingly that none other could possibly have been considered for leadership.

What manner of man was Jardine? It is best to take a good look at that interesting topic before trying to worry your head about the strange series now popularly known as the bodyline series and wonder what it was that caused them to flare up into the historic cricket event of the century. Jardine to my mind was a modern-day Hannibal. He led his team like an army, demanding absolute obedience and with rigid on-field discipline.

From a safe position outside the boundary fence it was not difficult to see that the lanky, red-faced, long-nosed man with the cap of many colours was the leader of the band. Seldom did Jardine seek helpful advice from fielding team-mates, although Herbert Sutcliffe was never loth to try to give it. It was never easy—in fact, going further, it was always downright difficult—for the onlooker to realise that the quiet-spoken, reserved Bob Wyatt was the deputy to the big boss.

When Iftikar Ali, the Nawab of Pataudi, carried on the tradition of Indian princes, scoring a first-up century for England in Tests against Australia it would have been safe to say that that young gentleman was to play a big part in that series from Sydney onward. The Nawab was omitted from the line-up immediately after the Melbourne Test, the second of the series, for disciplinary reasons. He refused to move across to a place in the leg field after the Australian captain had been floored.

Discipline with Jardine was the keynote of success. There was no place for anybody in his side who was not fully prepared to go along with him in his policy which was later to be roundly condemned throughout the cricket world.

I claim that he was a modern Hannibal. He could have led his team of elephants across the Rhone without great difficulties, even though he could not lead Pataudi across the pitch.

In Brisbane in the vital fourth Test he sent a taxi along to get Eddie Paynter out of the hospital bed in which he was sleeping off a painful attack of laryngitis so that he could bat England out of serious trouble—which little Eddie did.

During that same game Jardine, realising that the Australian selectors in their panic had dropped Clarrie Grimmett only to make his replacement Bert Tobin twelfth man, and had thereby played right into his hands, took 92 minutes to score his first run when he opened the batting with Sutcliffe. He knew he had the Australians euchred if he

painstakingly took the sting out of the remains of the attack. In doing that I suppose one could have sidestepped the allusion to Hannibal and fallen back upon Attila who left no doubt in anybody's mind that nothing of any real value should be left standing.

At the end of that patient innings I came face to face with the great man (on the verandah, fresh from the shower) smothering his manliness in an out-sized towel as he keenly observed the efforts of Jack Farquhar applying the mini-covers allowable those days for putting the pitch to bed for the night. Facetiously addressing him with "Well played, Douglas," I got the answer I deserved. "Really, Bill, really! Don't you think I was like an old maid defending her virginity?"

Jardine knew that Australians right round the cricket concourse hated the very sight of him—and he didn't care a damn. I knew him well later in his life and got a tremendous surprise to find that he was a pleasant host, a witty, reserved personality, who could make and hold friends—attributes which I had never even suspected back in 1932 when I had but one expressive word in my vocabulary to use when describing him.

Which leads me to the story of Robert Menzies' London dinner in honour of Mr Morrison, Speaker of the House of Commons, later to become Lord Dunrussil and a tragically short-lived Governor-General of Australia. As a grateful member of the guest list I found myself seated between Jardine and Gubby Allen with Freddie Brown sitting opposite—three ex-English captains and all present on the bodyline tour together. I was kept busy as you might imagine flying the Australian flag.

In a typically brilliant speech Bob suggested that he himself was more popular in England than at home, and that the thousands upon thousands who referred to him there as "Pig Iron Bob" hated him so much that they probably thought he was the biggest bastard ever to set foot in their country. It was then that Jardine and I agreed wholeheartedly for probably the first time in the evening when he said, "The honorable speaker is entirely misinformed; he could never possibly be better than number two."

Jardine was an outstanding leader of men. He set out to do a job and he did it thoroughly. His old school master and English cricketer of the twenties, Rockley Wilson, who knew Jardine as a schoolboy captain at Winchester College, on hearing that his "old boy" has been chosen to lead England in 1932 was heard to say, "We'll win the Ashes all right, but will probably lose a dominion."

I have never forgiven that man Douglas Jardine I met in Australia in 1932, but I have many happy memories of the one who bore the same name and was a valued friend in England in 1948 and 1953.

In 1923 I was taught ancient history at St Patrick's College, Goulburn, by a young science graduate from Queensland named Johnny Lynam. He was a magnificent young footballer who had represented the Australian Combined Universities in Rugby and was our idol. The last time I saw him was in 1946 at Brisbane, where he was a learned man of the law. Clarrie Grimmett and I had lunch with him at the Gabba on the day of that famous "catch or no catch" incident with Don Bradman, Bill Voce and John Ikin. When a

journalist named Philip Derriman introduced himself to me in the press box a few years ago I felt I had known him before —for, indeed, he was Johnny Lynam's nephew. Philip Derriman is now a distinguished colleague, and I am delighted to introduce his book.

Bill O'Reilly

Introduction

The text of this book first appeared as a series of articles in *The Sydney Morning Herald* in December, 1982. They were meant to coincide with the 50th anniversary of the 1932–33 series between England and Australia, and 50 years was reckoned to be time enough for even such controversial events to settle into their place in history. Happily, there were found to be at least a dozen survivors of that series available to supply personal recollections, and all of them, it seemed, were not only sharp of eye and robust of health but were remarkably clear in their memory of those distant events. It was apparent that the summer of 1932–33 had made as deep an impression on them personally as it had on the game's history. Several of them were extraordinarily generous with their time, and to them I am most grateful. They include Gubby Allen, who was kind enough to check the articles for accuracy, Bill O'Reilly, Bob Wyatt, Bill Bowes, Bill Ponsford and Les Ames. Harold Larwood assisted with a few reminiscences and Sir Donald Bradman provided helpful advice.

There are others who deserve the special gratitude of the *Herald* and myself. Mrs Fianach Lawry, Douglas Jardine's daughter, was extremely kind to the Australian journalist who sought her out at her home in Scotland in November, 1982. She provided a valuable insight into the character of her father, whom she remembers with deep affection. Dr Brian Stoddart, a Canberra historian whose years of research into the bodyline story have established him as one of the leading authorities on the subject, helped guide the research from which these articles were furnished. It was Dr Stoddart who several years ago provided us with a key to understanding the political ramifications of bodyline by uncovering the involvement of the Australian Prime Minister of the day, Joseph Lyons. He is still burrowing into the bodyline affair, and further revelations may yet be forthcoming.

It is a cause for much heart-burning at the *Herald* today that thousands of glass picture negatives were destroyed, deliberately, some 30 years ago. Fortunately, thousands of others were preserved, and nearly half the pictures in this book are printed from these old negatives. A sizeable proportion of them have not been printed in 50 years. Among the best of them are pictures taken by Herbert Fishwick, the celebrated press photographer before World War II. Born in England in 1882, Fishwick came to Sydney in 1905 and began working for the *Sydney Mail* and the *Herald* five years later. He was one of the first press photographers to use a telescopic lens, and the pictures he took in 1932–33 are of exceptional clarity. The *Herald*'s archivist, Eileen Dwyer, extracted all the glass negatives used for this book. John Manolato, with equal perseverence, printed them.

There are many more who gave freely of their time, expertise or knowledge. These are some of them, in no particular order: Hunter Hendry, Sir William McKell, Alan Barnes, the present Lord Gowrie, Arthur Morris, Legh Winser, Cliff Winning, Professor Ken Cable, Jack Egan, David Richards, John Arlott, David Clark, Bob Radford, Mrs Enid Austin, Fred Bennett, Richard Cashman, E.W. Swanton, Bill Mandle, Alan Dobbyn and the staffs of the Mitchell, National and Herald Libraries. The last of these were as forbearing as ever. Finally, thanks must go to Eric Beecher, whose idea it was in the first place.

Philip Derriman

EARLY ENCOUNTER

O N 24 May 1930, the touring Australian cricketers began their traditional fixture against Surrey at the Oval. It was the Australians' first match at the ground, so they would all have regarded it as important, but none more so than Don Bradman. His interest in it was special and personal, for he had a score to settle with the Surrey captain, Percy Fender.

A lot has been written about Bradman's capacity to take reprisals if his ability was questioned. Cricket writers have liked telling stories about it because it illustrated his remarkable competitiveness as well as his remarkable ability. Jack Fingleton, for instance, was fond of describing how Bradman went out of his way to murder the bowling of Arthur Mailey and Bert Ironmonger, both Test bowlers of the highest quality, after newspaper articles suggested they might have his measure. The great English bowler Maurice Tate suffered in the same way. When Bradman first got into the Australian team in 1928–29, Tate warned him that unless he played a straighter bat he would not be successful in England in 1930. 'What Bradman did to Tate in 1930,' the English writer Alan Gibson has noted, 'an Englishman can hardly bear to recollect.'

What makes Bradman's encounter with Percy Fender in 1930 so interesting is that our source for the story about it is Bradman himself. Fender has been in Australia in 1928–29 covering that season's Tests for two London newspapers, and in his articles and in a book he wrote afterwards he was consistently critical of the newcomer Bradman. The theme of his comments was that Bradman was brilliant but unsound. 'One minute one would think him a grand player,' he said, 'and the next he would look like a schoolboy.'

That Bradman resented Fender's criticism is evident from the fact that he referred to it in the two books he wrote about himself, one in 1931 and the other, long afterwards, in 1949. In the first of these, he wrote: 'I hope for pardon when I say I had a particularly personal reason for looking forward to my first match against Surrey. Mr Fender, the Surrey captain, besides being a great captain of a great county, is also a leading critic of his country; and if I have not misunderstood him, he did not think too highly of my batting or my fielding.'

If Fender, remembering and perhaps by then regretting his remarks about Bradman, had any apprehensions about opposing him for the first time on the field, they were soon shown to be well founded.

Australia batted first, and the early dismissal of one of the openers brought Bradman to the crease at 12.45 pm. It was an overcast day, and Bradman batted without a cap, as he often did early in his career. He began slowly enough, his caution probably reflecting his determination. He took ninety minutes to make his first 50.

At about that stage of his innings, as if he had concluded there was nothing to fear from the pitch, the light, the Surrey attack or Fender's stratagems, Bradman set upon the bowling with a ferocity which was exceptional even for him. He went from 50 to 100 in less than an hour and from 100 to 200 in only eighty minutes. At the end of the day he was unbeaten on 252, his only error having been a chance to short leg when his score was 207. When he returned to the Australian dressing room, he is reported to have said: 'I wonder what Fender will have to say in the morning paper this time.' (Edward Docker quoted this remark in his book, *Bradman and the Bodyline Series* — a book which Sir Donald Bradman approved for accuracy.)

Fender was considered to be a superb tactician. One writer called him the best English captain never to captain England. In that match against the Australians, he tried to contain Bradman with off theory, that is, by packing the offside field and directing his bowlers to pitch on or outside the off stump. Bradman's answer was to pull offside deliveries to mid-wicket. Fender moved a man from the covers to block the shot, and almost immediately Bradman drove through the covers where the fieldsman had been. 'I am not gloating,' Bradman wrote in his book, '... but I did feel that if this innings had not put me on my feet as far as Mr Fender was concerned, I at least felt satisfied.'

For Fender, then 37 years old and nearing the end of a distinguished career, it must have been a humbling experience. He had been made to look foolish by the 21-year-old Australian whose technique he had judged to be inferior. Bradman, we may be sure, let him know at the time that the innings was intended to square accounts.

Bradman's 252 not out at the Oval (the rest of the match was washed out, so Bradman did not get a chance to take his score beyond 300) was a highly impressive demonstration of his powers. It confirmed the fears of England's bowlers that a batsman of phenomenal talent had appeared on the scene.

Although not yet 22 years old, Bradman had shown he had the ability to score more prolifically than any batsman before him had dreamt of. By the time he arrived in England in 1930, his batting average in a first-class career not yet three years old was 90·04 and rising rapidly. In January 1930, he had set a world record for first-class cricket by scoring 452 not out for New South Wales against Queensland. His 252 not out against Surrey was only a foretaste of what the English bowlers had in store for them that summer. In seven Test innings he scored a century, two double centuries and a triple century for an average of 139·1 for the series.

It was batting of a kind that had never been seen before — brilliant but never wild, dynamic but always controlled. Neville Cardus was one of several English commentators who saw Bradman on his first tour in 1930 and marvelled that anyone so young could score at 50 runs an hour, for hour after hour, without once playing a rash stroke.

English bowlers had a better appreciation than anyone of Bradman's amazing ability. One of them, Bill Bowes, played against Bradman for the first time in 1930 and decided he was not merely head and shoulders above any other batsman he had seen. He was better, says Bowes, from the ankles up.

It would be interesting to know what impression Bradman's 252 not out at the Oval made on Fender, but it seems Fender never recorded his opinion of the innings. It would be even more interesting to know what impression the innings made on one of Fender's players, Douglas Jardine, who was on the field that day and was no doubt made to do a lot of running about by Bradman. Jardine was a friend and admirer of Fender, as well as being a fellow amateur. He had already acquired a distaste for Australians and their manners, and he could not have enjoyed the spectacle of Don Bradman, whom he might well have regarded as a brash upstart, making merry on the field at the expense of his captain.

Jardine also had a fine cricket brain, attuned to recognizing the strengths and weaknesses of opposing players, and he must have been deeply impressed by Bradman's mastery of the Surrey bowlers that day.

Then aged 29, Jardine had played against Australia in one series of Tests, in 1928–29, and, although he was unavailable for the Tests in 1930, he certainly had ambitions to play Test cricket against Australia again. Perhaps by then he was already considering the prospect of one day captaining England, and if so Bradman must immediately have loomed large in his considerations.

Jardine was, of course, to become the central character in the bodyline story. We will never know what first set his mind working on the problem of finding a counter to Bradman, but there is every possibility it was Bradman's 252 not out against Surrey.

Jardine had seen Bradman get a few centuries in Australia, but Bradman probably made no greater impact on him then than he did on Percy Fender, sitting in the press box. The match at the Oval gave Jardine his first experience of the Bradman run-making machine operating at full blast. We do not know if he saw Bradman make another big score that summer.

There is just a possibility, too, given the personal motive behind Bradman's assault on Fender's bowlers, that during this innings Jardine conceived a dislike for the young Australian. There is some evidence that Jardine felt a particular antipathy towards Bradman, although some of the men who played under him will deny that today. What may be said with certainty is that Jardine later adopted a highly combative attitude towards him.

JARDINE

DOUGLAS Jardine was a man of strange contrasts. In Australia he was seen as an archetypal upper-crust Englishman, yet he was Scottish by extraction and certainly looked upon himself as a Scotsman rather than an Englishman. As a youth he sometimes wore a kilt, and although he raised his children in the south of England he gave them all Scottish names. His three daughters were named Fianach, Marian Eillenagh and Iona and his only son was named Euan. He even had a pet Scottish name, Isla, for his wife Margaret.

His nationality was further complicated by the fact that he was born in Bombay of a distinguished colonial family. His grandfather had served as a judge in India and his father, M. R. Jardine, was a prominent lawyer there. However, it seems that Jardine, an only child, spent little of his boyhood in India. His parents sent him to school in England while he was still a small boy, first to a preparatory school called Horris Hill and then to one of the country's most exclusive schools, Winchester. Most of his holidays were spent with his maternal grandmother at St Andrews in Scotland.

It must have been a lonely upbringing, and the extent to which it determined the kind of man he became can only be guessed at. One of his daughters, Mrs Fianach Lawry, who was 22 when her father died remembers him well, thinks Jardine was to an abnormal extent a product of his boyhood. It taught him to be a survivor, she says, but it also made him a loner.

She thinks the influence of Winchester, with its code of the stiff upper lip, was particularly strong. He emerged from it a complex, introverted character. 'I think a lot went on underneath the surface that didn't necessarily come out,' she says. 'For this is the way Winchester worked in those days. The silences and the things he didn't say perhaps made people feel he was a hard man. The idea was not to let anyone see that you were hurt or upset. He was bad at communicating in today's terms, but there again we're back to Winchester. I think Winchester has a lot to answer for.'

Although Jardine's success as a cricketer had been attributed to practice and application rather than to an abundance of talent, there is no doubt he excelled at the game from his earliest years. At Winchester, he was outstanding both as a player and as a captain. The noted cricket commentator and historian, H. S. Altham, who was a master at Winchester, said Jardine was about the best boy captain he ever saw.

But even at Winchester he showed he could be abrasive. Recently one of his contemporaries there wrote to Paul Wheeler, the scriptwriter for the movie on the bodyline series, to tell him of an incident which made Jardine highly unpopular with a team he was captaining at Winchester. The team had only two good cricketers, Jardine and one other boy, and before one match, when Jardine posted the names in the team up on the notice board, he listed only the two of them as having been chosen to play. Immediately under their names, however, he wrote: 'The following nine boys (their names were then supplied) have also been chosen to appear even though they cannot bat, bowl or field to save their lives' — or words to that effect.

Incidents of this kind have made Wheeler conclude that Jardine thrived on unpopularity or, as he puts it, that 'Jardine must have got some kind of adrenalin out of being disliked'. According to Wheeler, Jardine sometimes seemed to force people to dislike him. It is an interesting observation and one worth considering in any analysis of Jardine's behaviour during the bodyline Tests.

From Winchester, Jardine went to Oxford, where in his first year he won his blue for cricket, as his father had done 30 years earlier. Unlike his father, however, Jardine was never made captain of Oxford. According to someone I have spoken to who knew Jardine well in his playing days, this was probably because he was considered at Oxford to be a 'difficult' person. The euphemism 'difficult' is one you often hear used to describe Jardine by people who knew him.

By this time Jardine had developed into a batsman of the first rank. He was reckoned to be as close to perfection in technique as it seemed possible for any batsman to be. A high left elbow was his hallmark. He was not quick on his feet and, although a long reach helped to compensate for this (he was about 6 feet 2 inches tall), he was consequently more at home to fast bowling than to slow spin. He was essentially a defensive player, and his defence was very strong. Neville Cardus wrote of him: 'If it is necessary for victory's sake for him to bat for an hour and make no runs — very well, then, Jardine will enjoy the grind of it all; the crowd can perish of boredom.'

Jardine was included in the English team which toured Australia in 1928–29, and he began the tour with striking success by scoring a century in each of his first three matches. Hunter (Stork) Hendry, who is today Australia's oldest Test cricketer, played for Victoria in the second of those matches. He tells a story about Jardine in that match which shows how quickly he had become antagonized by Australian barrackers. Jardine had got his century just before tea and Hendry had gone out of his way to congratulate him. The innings had been a typically slow one, but the Melbourne crowd had made few complaints. After tea, however, when Jardine failed to step up the scoring rate, the crowd became impatient.

'They really got at him — they started to give him hell,' Hendry says. 'I was fielding in slips only a yard or two from him. I said to him, "I hear the wolves are out," meaning the crowd. With that he turned around and said Australians were just bloody mongrels, and he obviously meant me included. I said, "If that's your opinion you can go to buggery." He was the only person I ever swore at on a cricket field.' I asked Hendry if Jardine had actually said 'mongrels'. He replied: 'He may not have used that word, but that was his meaning.'

Jardine was singled out by the Australian crowds for a great deal of personal abuse that summer. To some extent this was inevitable. His appearance, his manner, his slow batting and the multi-coloured Harlequin cap that he wore made him, in Jack Fingleton's words, 'a barracking gift from the gods'. Four years later when Jardine was letting his bodyline bowlers loose on Australian batsmen, Australians cast about for ways to explain his apparent animosity towards them. It was then that people remembered the barracking he had been subjected to in 1928–29. Although this was a convenient explanation, it may well have been the right one.

John Arlott, a friend of Jardine in his later years, believes that in his playing days Jardine associated Australians as a whole with Australian barrackers. 'And Australian barrackers disgusted him,' Arlott says.

It is only fair to say that some who knew Jardine, including his family and several survivors of his team, do not agree he had any underlying dislike of Australians, beyond a quite normal hostility towards them on the field. The weight of evidence, however, seems to be against them. Jardine's hostility towards Australians certainly extended beyond the field, although it may be true that it did not extend beyond the game. Pelham Warner, the manager of the English team on the bodyline tour, believed Jardine's attitude to Australians was at the heart of the bodyline controversy. 'He is a queer fellow,' Warner said in a personal letter in 1934. 'When he sees a cricket ground with an Australian on it he goes mad.'

The statement was made earlier that Jardine was a man of strange contrasts. This was especially true of his personality. To most Australians, he seemed an austere, humourless autocrat, who cared little for the feelings of other people when pursuing an objective. But there was another side to his nature which Jardine seems to have gone to some trouble to conceal. Many people who got to know him in later years, including former Australian players such as Bill O'Reilly, were surprised to find that he was actually an extremely shy man. Indeed, his daughter thinks his shyness was perhaps his most dominant personality trait. His 'iron side', she says, was essentially a shield for his shyness.

Some, but not all, of those close to him thought he had a keen sense of humour. John Arlott tells of meeting Jardine for the first time after the war. 'I went to see him and I was terrified,' Arlott says. 'I'd heard all the legends about this ruthless Scot. But in the first few sentences he made a few jokes and everything was all right. He was a witty man with a terribly dry sense of humour. He was very funny — he could paralyse you with laughter.'

Others who knew Jardine remember him today for his kindness, a virtue not often credited him in his playing days. Bob Wyatt, who was Jardine's vice-captain on the bodyline tour, says there was almost a Jekyll-and-Hyde dichotomy in Jardine's character. 'He actually had a very kind heart,' Wyatt says.

Wyatt had a revealing encounter with Jardine when they were visiting Manchester to see a cricket match after the war.

Wyatt was about to drive away from the Old Trafford ground one evening when he noticed Jardine walking past and offered him a lift to his hotel. With some reluctance Jardine accepted, but he remained evasive about where he was going. Eventually he said to Wyatt, 'Drop me at the next corner — I can walk from here,' but Wyatt insisted on driving him all the way. It was only then that Jardine told Wyatt that he was going to stay at the home of an elderly nurse who had been kind to him while he was in a military hospital during the war. 'The old girl is in a bad way financially,' Jardine said, 'and I'm going there as a PG [paying guest].' Wyatt says: 'He could have stayed at the best hotel in Manchester with his friends but he was doing some old nurse a good turn instead and didn't want anyone to know about it.'

A FATEFUL STEP

EARLY in 1931 the MCC appointed Douglas Jardine to captain England in the Tests that year against New Zealand. It was a fateful step, for from that time onwards, the strife and bitterness of 1932–33 were probably inevitable. The bomb that was almost to blow the cricket world apart was now ticking away.

The chairman of the selectors who recommended Jardine for the captaincy was Pelham ('Plum') Warner, a former captain of England himself, who was then a man of influence within the MCC. Warner's early patronage of Jardine is significant, in view of his subsequent disavowal of Jardine's tactics. In a book he wrote some years later, Warner made several interesting disclosures about Jardine's appointment as captain. One was that he, personally, had promoted Jardine's cause. Warner wrote: 'When in 1931 I came into closer contact with Jardine I realized — it was easy to do — that here was a man who was a thorough student of the game of cricket, keen and competent, one who had thought much and pondered deeply over the tactics and strategy of the game and, incidentally, a stern critic of his own cricketing abilities. The coming tour appeared to him in the light of a crusade, and it was certain that he would put his whole soul and endeavour into the work in front of him. Backed by my colleagues, I recommended him to the MCC committee in an appreciation of the situation which is, no doubt, in the archives of Lord's.'

Warner clearly wanted it known that he was chiefly responsible for Jardine's appointment. In case anyone should doubt that fact, he also let it be known that the archives at Lord's could verify it. (Theoretically, that is. This writer's personal experience suggests that such a document will not be prised out of Lord's for another 50 years at least.) The point Warner was probably trying to make was that he had put his trust in Jardine and that Jardine, by using bodyline tactics, later betrayed that trust. As we shall see, this was certainly how Warner viewed the matter.

But the most interesting part of the above excerpt from Warner's book is his statement that as early as 1931 Jardine viewed the coming tour of Australia in 1932–33 as a 'crusade'. What are we to make of this? It cannot mean simply that Jardine had his heart set on regaining the Ashes lost in 1930. Any prospective captain would have had that ambition. The word 'crusade' surely implies something more, that Jardine had dedicated himself to a special cause. That cause, undoubtedly, was to stop Don Bradman making runs.

If England's cricketers had entertained hopes that Bradman would not be able to maintain his astonishing rate of scoring, those hopes would probably have been abandoned by 1931 and certainly by 1932. At the start of the Australian summer of 1930–31 he had made a handful of moderate scores but then had peeled off three double centuries and two centuries in his last 12 innings of the season. In the 1931–32 season he batted only 13 times but made three double centuries and four centuries. His average in four Tests against the South Africans that season was 201·50. And he was still only 23 years old.

Any Englishman pondering his team's prospects in Australia in 1932–33 would have been able, with a few minutes of mental arithmetic, to work out that Bradman was scoring a century every second time he went to the wicket and that one in two of those centuries became a double century. Bradman's presence in the Australian team seemed to ensure that any attempt by England to regain the Ashes would be futile.

No English captain had ever been presented with an assignment as formidable as subduing Don Bradman in 1932–33. Yet it was a challenge that Jardine grasped eagerly, even before he had thought of how he might try to meet it. That was the nature of his crusade: to bring down the Australian Goliath with a slingshot, or by any other means that offered itself. Cricket was never to be the same again.

THE PLOT

THE abiding mystery of the bodyline story is how it all began. Was bodyline bowling the product of a conspiracy of English players and officials, perhaps including some of the top people at Lord's? Or was it the creation of one man, Douglas Jardine, the English captain who directed its use against Australian batsmen in the summer of 1932–33?

The conspiracy theory has a flimsy basis. Perhaps one day a document will be found in the archives at Lord's to prove the MCC had a hand in formulating bodyline, but at present the evidence for this is not convincing.

The main reason the MCC was suspected of complicity by some Australians was that it chose to include four fast bowlers in the team which sailed for Australia in September 1932. Today this would be considered normal selection policy, but 50 years ago, when much more reliance was placed on medium pace and spin, it immediately made Australian batsmen wonder if something special was in store for them. 'It seemed obvious that we were to be subjected to a battery of fast bowling,' Don Bradman wrote, 'although the precise nature of it could not, at that stage, have been foreseen.'

It is reasonable to speculate that Pelham Warner and the two other selectors were encouraged by Jardine to pick four fast bowlers, for by then his plans for a fast leg theory attack were well advanced. Harold Larwood is sure the selectors knew of Jardine's plans. 'There had never been four speed merchants sent to Australia before,' he noted in his book *The Larwood Story*. On the other hand, Gubby Allen, another of those four fast bowlers, doubts that Jardine ever told the selectors of his intentions. 'Having four fast bowlers was not so surprising,' he says. 'There wasn't a lot [of other bowling talent] around.'

I have recently spoken to most of the members of Jardine's team still living. Although their account of the origins of bodyline varied in detail, it was hard not to come to the following conclusions:
- The bodyline ideas was probably conceived by and certainly developed by Jardine himself;
- It was not brought to Australia as a master plan for victory — it had been sketched in only broad outlines in Jardine's mind when the tour got under way;
- It was only when the idea proved a success in its initial trials that Jardine decided to adopt it as his team's main bowling strategy; and
- Its primary purpose was to curb the scoring of Don Bradman.

What put the idea in Jardine's mind? Here, one enters an area of conjecture and contradiction. The most popular theory, and one widely endorsed on the English side, is that while making 232 in the fifth Test at the Oval in 1930, Bradman seemed unsettled by fast, rising deliveries from Harold Larwood during one brief period when the pitch was damp and the ball kept rearing. 'Don didn't like the balls rising on his body,' Larwood wrote. 'He kept drawing away.'

Legend has it that the English wicket-keeper, George

Duckworth, noticed Bradman's discomfort and mentioned it afterwards to Jardine, who began at once trying to think of ways to exploit the apparent weakness. Bradman, it ought to be noted, has disputed the English claim that he was unhappy against Larwood's bowling that day at the Oval. On the other hand, Gubby Allen, who was in Jardine's team but is well disposed to Bradman, is 'pretty sure' he can remember English players discussing Bradman's dislike of the lifting deliveries at the time.

Jardine is also said to have got advice and inspiration from two of England's leading tacticians of the day — Percy Fender, the captain of Surrey until Jardine replaced him in March 1932, and Arthur Carr, the captain of Nottinghamshire. Jardine had a high regard for Fender as a strategist, once describing him as possessing the 'ablest, the quickest and the most enterprising cricket brain' he had known. According to at least two sources, it was Fender who first suggested to Jardine that he should try using some kind of leg theory against Bradman and the other Australians. Fender himself denied this, but there is no doubt Jardine spent many hours discussing tactics with him before the tour.

The part played by Arthur Carr is more intriguing still. Some Australian players suspected that he was in fact the mastermind in the bodyline plot, but Carr made it clear this was not so. We must take his word for it, for he was a supporter of bodyline and would have been proud to claim the credit for inventing it. This is also true, incidentally, of Fender.

Carr and Jardine had a good deal in common. Both had backgrounds of privilege (Carr was at Eton until the school expelled him), both were amateur cricketers, ostensibly playing for the fun of it, and yet both had a tough, professional approach to the game. Opponents were not given, nor expected to give, any quarter. Carr was not at all squeamish about using bodyline himself. 'The game was never intended for namby-pambies,' he once wrote.

Carr and Jardine also shared a dislike of Australians. Carr wrote: 'My own experience of the Australians is that if they cannot win they will not stand to be beaten if they can help it or avoid it. They will go to almost any length to dodge defeat ... To the Australians cricket is a business almost pure and simple — a matter of money — and success is all that matters to them.' He said there were only two Australian cricketers he knew that he would give twopence for, Charlie Macartney and Arthur Mailey. 'A pity that more of the Australians who get into big cricket are not built as Mailey is built,' he wrote. 'If there were more like him the Australians would be more popular here than they are ... You need not wear an old school tie or a Harlequin cap to have good manners.'

Carr believed Australians had always played the game hard, and he saw bodyline as a just and overdue response by England. It seems this attitude was fairly common among Englishmen at the time. Their feeling was that for too long England had been led by gentlemen captains who concentrated on winning popularity while the Australians concentrated on winning Tests. As Neville Cardus said: 'A number of English captains of cricket have wasted their public school amenities on heroes whose greatness had come out of a hearty appreciation of things as they are. A national game simply will not be confined in cotton wool.' Jardine was seen as a welcome break from this tradition.

At Carr's direction, the two Notts fast bowlers, Larwood and Bill Voce, had used leg theory from time to time since 1931. Their example was followed by several other fast bowlers in England, most notably Bill Bowes of Yorkshire, who not only used leg theory against Jack Hobbs in a match against Surrey in August 1932, but bounced the ball repeatedly at Hobbs' head. Pelham Warner condemned Bowes' bouncers in the paper next day, saying, 'That is not bowling. Indeed, it is not cricket.' This statement was to be thrown up at Warner again and again during the bodyline crises in Australia a few months later.

Carr, then, was England's leading authority on fast leg theory, and when he brought the Notts team to London to play Surrey late in the English summer of 1932, Jardine sought him out to ask for advice. The request was actually conveyed by Percy Fender. Carr later recalled: 'He (Fender) gave me the tip that Jardine wanted to learn more about my two bowlers, Larwood and Voce, and proposed to ask the two bowlers and myself out to dinner to discuss things. We all went to the grill room at the Piccadilly Hotel.'

Larwood has given a detailed account of the conversation at dinner that night. According to Larwood, Jardine revealed he had a plan to use fast leg theory against Bradman in Australia and he asked for the opinion of the two bowlers, who had by then been chosen for the tour. Both were in favour of it. Shortly after this, Jardine called on the former English fast bowler, Frank Foster, and obtained from him the field placings he had used when bowling leg theory in Australia in 1911-12. Jardine's preparations for his great undertaking were now complete.

Up to this point, the development of the bodyline concept seems easy enough to follow. As early as 1931, when he becomes captain of England, Jardine starts looking ahead to the tour of Australia in 1932-33 and ponders the necessity of finding some novel means of countering Bradman. Eventually he considers the idea of using some kind of fast leg theory against him, perhaps because Bradman seemed disconcerted by Larwood's lifting deliveries at the Oval in 1930. He consults Fender, who encourages him in the idea, and finally consults Carr and two of the fast bowlers chosen for the tour.

But after this the course of events is not so easy to understand. Having gone to a lot of trouble to devise a new bowling plan, Jardine seems then to have kept the plan largely to himself. Even his vice-captain, Bob Wyatt, insists today that Jardine did not give him an inkling of it until some time after their arrival in Australia. Larwood wrote that Jardine 'outlined his method of attack to the other fast bowlers' during the voyage out, but he seems to be in error here, for the other fast bowlers, Allen and Bowes, assure me that Jardine did not say a word to them about it on the ship.

Since plans for a movie about bodyline were first announced, Gubby Allen has had long discussions with three other survivors of Jardine's team, Wyatt, Freddie Brown and Les Ames. 'We've thrashed over bodyline like the devil this summer,' Allen says. Having thus refreshed his memories of bodyline, this is how he views the question of its origins today:

'It is my belief that Douglas never formed a positive plan at that stage [before the team arrived in Australia]. The whole thing was really how were they going to keep Bradman quiet. If they're going to tell me, as certain people have written, that the whole plan was made in England, I won't believe a word of it. You mean to tell me they had thrashed out bodyline, or what came to be known as bodyline, and nobody ever talked about it on the boat? We four will go to our graves saying we never once heard it mentioned on the boat. Now I can't believe that if this plot had been really hatched in England it could never have been once mentioned on the boat.'

In other words, Jardine did not bother talking to his team about his leg theory strategy because it was no more than a rough plan which he hoped to test if the right opportunity arose. For all we know, he may have been highly pessimistic about its chances of success.

The spearhead of his attack, Harold Larwood, might not have inspired him with a lot of confidence. Larwood had toured Australia four years before with only moderate success. Since then, in 1930, he had taken such a terrific pounding from Bradman that he was actually dropped for one Test. He was now 28 years old, an age at which most fast bowlers have ceased to improve and are happy enough to maintain the form they once had. Indeed, there had been some doubt Larwood would be chosen for the tour.

Imagine Jardine's joy at discovering after their arrival in Australia that Larwood was a couple of yards faster than he had ever been. His speed, always impressive, was now tremendous. Jardine had the weapon he needed to wage his bodyline campaign.

BRADMANIA

BY the summer of 1932–33, the Australian public's interest in Don Bradman had attained the proportions of a craze. He filled cricket grounds whenever he played, and from October to March he filled the columns of the sports pages. It was a phenomenon which people came to call Bradmania.

The English journalist William Pollock visited Australia in the 1930s and afterwards wrote: 'Australia is Bradman mad. You hear his name all day long in the mouths of men, women and children in the cricket season. Everything he says or does — or is supposed to say or do — is seized upon... People who know nothing about cricket go to see him bat, women in particular.'

Pollock's reference to women is interesting, because it seems there is a story still untold about Bradman's appeal to women. A recent article in the London *Observer,* apparently quoting English sources, tells of women fighting to kiss him or touch his sleeve. Newspapers made few, if any, references to this side of Bradman's attraction at the time, perhaps because it would have been considered indiscreet to do so. There is no doubt that cricket crowds in the 1930s contained a much higher proportion of women than today, though to what extent Bradman was responsible for this is a matter for conjecture.

It is interesting today to study pictures taken of Bradman as he emerged from the crowd on his way to the wicket. The eyes of the spectators are fixed on him and their faces shine with excitement and anticipation. Their faces reveal more about the way Australians revered Bradman than do pages of statistics on how he lifted gate receipts.

There is no mystery about the appeal Bradman made to those spectators. The reason for it was simply, that he was extraordinarily good. He was not flamboyant, far from it, and he made no attempt to court public favour. People went specially to see him because they knew that when they paid their shilling or two shillings at the turnstiles they had a 50-50 chance, literally, of seeing him make a century and a chance of one in four of seeing him make a double century. This was true in the early 1930s, but his rate of century-scoring did drop a little as he got older. Over his 21-year career in first-class cricket, Bradman on average scored a century every 2·88 times he went in to bat.

Moreover, he scored his runs at a speed which seems scarcely credible today. It is not sufficient to say that Bradman scored at 40 or 50 an hour, for, as critics of modern cricket have noted frequently in recent years, bowlers in Bradman's day bowled many more balls an hour than they do today. The only fair way to measure Bradman's rate of scoring is by the ratio of runs scored to balls faced. Fortunately, there are statistics available which enable us to do this.

Judged by this yardstick, Bradman's scoring rate is still impressive. Even though he played sedately in several Test innings in 1930, his 974 runs in the series were scored off only 1,580 balls. This means he scored about 3·7 runs for every six balls faced, which is half as fast again as the scoring rates of most batsmen in the 1982–83 Test series. Some English bowlers in 1930 suffered more than others. Off Harold Larwood, Bradman scored at the remarkable rate of 5·6 runs for every six balls faced.

For all that, Bradman's popularity was certainly a product of the age and, in particular, of the Depression. In recent years, Australian historians have become increasingly conscious of the historical importance of cricket as a focus of national aspirations. I know of five academics in Sydney and Canberra alone who are interested in the subject. Bradman makes a fascinating study for them, for he was an object of intense national pride at a time when national morale was low.

One hesitates to make the rather trite observation that Bradman was a symbol of hope for a country stricken by the Depression, but he may have been something close to that. He certainly provided Australians with cheering news far more often than any other individual did in those years when the Depression was at its worst, 1930 to 1932.

Professor Ken Cable, of the Sydney University history department, believes Australians in the Depression years warmed to Bradman because they saw him as a little Aussie battler who had made good. He was a cheeky boy from the bush who had run rings around the best cricketers England could muster and grinned while he was doing it. According to Professor Cable, success against England at cricket was important to Australians' self esteem because Australians tended always to measure themselves against Englishmen. And Bradman was the embodiment of success.

The Hollywood-star treatment Bradman had been receiving since 1930 was a cause of irritation, and in some cases jealousy, among his Australian team-mates. Jack Fingleton has described how deflating it was to be batting with Bradman when he got out and to see a sizeable proportion of the crowd leave immediately, uninterested in anything the other Australian batsmen might do.

There was at least one Englishman irritated by it all, too — Douglas Jardine, the English captain. He wrote the following after experiencing Bradmania in 1932–33:

'Few will be found to admit that the hero-worship, almost amounting to idolatry, to which, for example, Bradman was subject, is desirable for the game's good, or fair to the individual. It encouraged the view that Bradman was a run-making machine of almost superhuman powers — in short, that he was a team in himself; and this habit of extolling one man must naturally lead to the lack of appreciation of others.'

It is likely that this comment by Jardine was prompted neither by his concern for the game's good nor by any concern for the Australian players whom Bradman had put in the shade. Rather, it was prompted by a hostility towards Bradman that is evident in almost everything Jardine wrote about him.

THE UNVEILING

THE tour by Jardine's men began uneventfully. After their arrival at Fremantle, the England team manager, Pelham Warner, and Jardine made the usual speeches, expressing the hope the tour would strengthen bonds between Britain and Australia. In a message to all Australians, Jardine said: 'I hope that the visit of the present team will create as much interest and good feeling as has been the case with past sides. Both England and Australia have been passing through difficult times in a manner worthy of our race ... May the friendly rivalry, our joint national pastime, add its quota of cement to the foundation laid in the past.'

The Englishmen played a match at Perth against a Combined Eleven, including Bradman, but their bowling tactics were perfectly orthodox. Bradman failed twice in that match, scoring 3 and 10, but he batted on a rain-affected pitch, so his failures did not attract special comment. There was more interest at the time in a controversy over whether a newspaper contract would prevent him playing in the Tests, a controversy which was soon to fizzle out.

According to Jack Fingleton, Bradman told him while they were playing golf before the match in Perth that he suspected that the Englishmen considered him vulnerable to pace. 'Bradman knew then what was up the English sleeve,' Fingleton wrote. But he did not know then of Jardine's bodyline plan. Nor, apparently, did most of the English team.

As we have seen, Bill Bowes, the tall, bespectacled, fast-medium bowler from Yorkshire, used tactics akin to bodyline in a match against Surrey shortly before the Englishmen sailed for Australia. It is reasonable to assume, then, that he was one of the first English players, after Larwood and Voce, to be informed of Jardine's new bowling strategy. Yet Bowes insists today he knew nothing of the bodyline plan until the team was playing in Adelaide.

Even then he virtually had to force Jardine to tell him. During the match against South Australia, Jardine had suggested to Bowes that he should bowl to a legside field but had refused to explain to him the strategy behind the idea. Bowes was naturally indignant, and it was only after a heated exchange with Jardine in the English dressing room that evening that Jardine took him into his confidence. He told Bowes he wanted to try fast leg theory against Bradman and the other Australians because he believed the English bowlers had no hope against them otherwise.

The Englishmen moved on to Melbourne, and there, at last, the fast leg theory trap was sprung. In the match against Victoria, Voce bowled aggressively with three men in short-leg positions, but it caused little concern.

A few days later the Englishmen began a match in Melbourne against an Australian XI. Bradman was in the team, and the Englishmen decided to field all four of their fast bowlers, thereby confirming Bradman's suspicions that they hoped to overcome him with pace. Bodyline tactics of a rudimentary sort were used against the two openers, so by the time Bradman came to the crease at the fall of the first wicket he knew exactly what he was up against.

From the outset it was clear he intended meeting the challenge head-on. He took 13 off one over from Bowes, but then Larwood was brought on at Bowes's end. It was the first time Bradman had faced Larwood that season, and, according to newspaper accounts next day, the significance of the encounter was not lost on the huge Melbourne crowd.

Larwood's first ball to Bradman was short, and Bradman stepped back and crashed it to the point boundary, producing, we are told, 'shrieks of delight' from the crowd. The second ball was a bouncer, which Bradman chose to duck. The next ball was also short, but Bradman hooked it in spectacular fashion for another four. Then an ominous development: all but one of the slips fieldsmen moved across to take up positions on the legside. A few overs later Bradman was trapped lbw by Larwood for 36. In the second innings he was bowled by Larwood for 13, while pulling away to cut. In both innings Larwood was reported, in the parlance of the day, to have repeatedly made the ball 'fly' at the Australian batsman.

Bradman wrote later that he recognized bodyline for what it was when he first saw it in that match at Melbourne. 'Its purport was obvious to me,' he said. 'I promptly confided to responsible officials my predictions regarding the future, but found little sympathy for my views.'

The English tactics made little impression, however, on the Australian press. Newspapers noted with displeasure the use of a legside field and at least one accused Larwood of intimidatory bowling, but in general the criticism was mild.

The most curious feature of that first trial of Jardine's bodyline tactics was that Jardine himself was not present to witness the results. He had gone trout fishing in the Kiewa River at Tawonga, near Albury, and had left his deputy, Bob Wyatt, to captain the team. The fact that it was Wyatt who stationed four men behind square leg while the fast bowlers were repeatedly making the ball lift, seems to provide proof that Jardine had by now involved his whole team in the bodyline plot.

However, Wyatt later wrote a book in which he claimed to have set that legside field in Melbourne on his own initiative, without instructions from Jardine. Now in his eighties and living in retirement near the tip of Cornwall, Wyatt still stands by that assertion. 'It was quite obvious Bradman did not like the field placing,' he says. 'It worried him. When Jardine got back from his fishing trip I told him about it. He said, 'Oh, that's interesting. We'll have to give him more of it".'

Wyatt says he moved the slips across not to intimidate the batsmen but to stop them getting easy runs on the onside. Because the legside field seemed to disconcert Bradman, the English selection committee afterwards discussed its possibilities and out of this, according to Wyatt, emerged bodyline. 'I am absolutely certain the whole thing gradually evolved,' Wyatt says. 'I think it evolved from that [Melbourne] field setting.'

Wyatt's account does not sit easily with the rest of the bodyline story as we know it, but he is certainly correct in saying that bodyline was still evolving. In the weeks ahead it developed into a more fearsome and effective method of attack.

It is probably true that it was the success of Wyatt's tactics in Melbourne which persuaded Jardine to adopt fast leg theory/bodyline as his principal bowling strategy. The key to that strategy was, of course, Harold Larwood. Fortunately, enough newsreel footage has survived to show that Larwood's contemporaries were not exaggerating when they wrote rapturously of the rhythm and power of his bowling action.

Bill Bowes says Larwood's bowling in 1932–33 acquired what he describes as a ricochet effect. He says Larwood's deliveries did not seem to bounce so much as to skim off the pitch, like a pebble skimming off water. Any ball delivered by Larwood was therefore quite likely to take off towards a batsman's throat from only just short of a length. Another ball of the same length was just as likely to come through below bail height. Bowes attributes this effect to Larwood's tremendous speed that summer, to the hard Australian wickets and to his low trajectory (Larwood was only about 5 feet 8 inches tall).

Realising the necessity of keeping Larwood fit, Jardine began detailing a couple of his team at the end of each day's play to look after him and make sure he did not drink too much or stay out too late. Bill Bowes sometimes acted as Larwoods 'chaperon'. I asked him if Larwood was drinking a lot after his exertions on the field. He replied: 'No, he wasn't drinking a lot. But it didn't take much. You know, two or three glasses of beer and he was quite prepared to sing.'

From Melbourne, the Englishmen travelled to Sydney and used bodyline against New South Wales. Larwood was not playing, but Voce gave the batsmen a torrid time. Voce was not exceptionally fast — Bill O'Reilly says he bowled at about Terry Alderman's pace — but he was able to make the ball rear nastily up and into a right-handed batsman. (It is interesting to speculate whether the Australians might have fared better against bodyline if all its leading batsmen had not been right-handed.) Jack Fingleton, a New South Wales opener, carried his bat and made 119, but, as he wrote later, he took no pleasure in it.

'I was conscious of a hurt,' he said, 'and it was not because of the physical pummelling I had taken from Voce. It was the consciousness of a crashed ideal. Playing against England in actuality had proved vastly different from what boyish dreams and adventure had imagined it to be.' Fingleton's mother watched that match and was so upset by what she saw that she refused to go back to the Sydney Cricket Ground to watch another, even when her son made his Test debut against England a week later.

Bradman failed again in the New South Wales match, making only 18 and 23. In the second innings, he moved towards the off to avoid what he apparently thought was going to be a bouncer from Voce, only to have his middle stump knocked over behind his back. In six innings against Jardine's men he had made only 103 runs. Something seemed to have gone very wrong with his batting. 'I knew I had Don on the run,' Larwood wrote. 'I knew I had Don rattled.'

Fingleton said it was at this stage of the English tour that relations soured between English and Australian players. Initially, Englishmen fielding close to the wicket offered sympathy to Australian batsmen when they were hit, but gradually they stopped doing this. Soon, the opposing players gave up talking to each other at all.

It was at Sydney, too, that Australian crowds began to take strong objection to the English tactics and shout abuse at the English players. The controversy was hotting up, but still the newspapers gave it low-key treatment.

This slowness of the Australian papers to bring the controversy into the open is one of the most puzzling features of the bodyline story. From the time the English tactics were first unveiled in Melbourne, there was always a good story to be picked up from the home side's dressing room, yet the weeks went by without the story being written. Tom Goodman, who covered the series for *The Sydney Morning Herald,* says one reason (at least in the case of his own paper) was that the editors back at the office simply could not bring themselves to believe that an Englishman of Jardine's background would do anything unfair. Some Australians, although not many editors, persisted in this belief to the end.

For the time being, the main interest for the newspapers was Bradman's loss of form. Asked about his prospects against the English fast bowlers in the coming Tests, Bradman was reported to have said: 'Don't worry . . . I will be as right as pie.'

STORMS GATHER

IF JARDINE had misgivings about the fairness of his tactics, he did not ever reveal them. On the contrary: the more bodyline was condemned, the more relentlessly he employed it. Jardine's vice-captain, Bob Wyatt, has told me that Jardine used to say the Australian batsmen were 'yellow', meaning cowardly. When a new Australian batsman was on his way to the crease after the fall of a wicket, Jardine would often make a derisive remark to the English fieldsmen such as: 'Here comes another yellow bastard'. The implication was that the Australians were not standing up to Harold Larwood's bowling manfully enough.

Of course, this may have been Jardine's way of psyching up his players. He would have sensed that many of them, possibly even a majority of them, felt uneasy about the ethics of bodyline, and perhaps he decided they needed mental toughening. He certainly tried to psych them up in the dressing room, especially when they had to get Bradman out. Gubby Allen recalls Jardine saying 'some pretty rough things about Don to stir us up'. According to another member of Jardine's team, if Bradman was in or about to come in Jardine would say to his men through clenched teeth: 'Come on — we've got to get the little bastard out.' Jardine had worse names for Bradman, which need not be repeated here.

The barracking began in earnest during the first Test at Sydney. Larwood and Voce bowled to the now familiar bodyline field. Voce, in particular, was abused by the Hill for repeatedly bowling bouncers. He hit Alan Kippax and Stan McCabe, and Larwood hit Vic Richardson. At least, these were the hits reported by the press. There were many others not reported. The Australian opening batsman Bill Ponsford, for instance, estimates he was hit 50 times during the series.

Don Bradman did not play in the first Test. On the eve of the match he was examined by two doctors and ruled unfit, although it was never made clear what he was suffering from. The doctors were reported to have told Australian cricket officials that he was 'organically sound' but was in a 'seriously run-down condition'. In his autobiography, Bradman said only that his health had 'deteriorated considerably,' although he did admit in the preceding paragraph that the 'strain of cricket and travel and argument' had begun to tell and was affecting his batting. Jardine believed Bradman had had a nervous breakdown. He said so in a book he wrote two years later.

If Bradman did suffer some kind of nervous strain, the cause would not be hard to find. For two years he had been the centre of publicity more intense than any Australian had experienced before or probably has experienced since. The pressure on him to meet the crowds' expectations of him must always have been tremendous, but never so tremendous as it was now, for the whole country looked to him to destroy Jardine's bodyline.

But the truth is probably that Bradman had already made up his mind that bodyline could not be mastered. He had worked out a method of trying to counter it — stepping away from his wicket and clubbing the ball into the vacant offside field — but he would have realized that unless he was extraordinarily lucky this could not succeed for long. The Australian public was confident he could accomplish what he himself guessed was beyond his powers — that was his difficulty. It would have caused stress and anxiety in the most hardened of veterans, and Bradman, remember, was barely 24.

Bill O'Reilly has a special regret about Bradman's absence from the team in the first Test. In the first innings of the Test, Stan McCabe played an innings which most cricket historians count among the most outstanding in the game's history. He scored 187 not out in 242 minutes, and for the whole of that time he was in command of the bodyline attack. O'Reilly believes that if Bradman had been in with McCabe, attacking the bowling at the other end, bodyline might never have been heard of again. He reasons that if bodyline bowling had been given a hammering by these two batsmen in Sydney, Jardine might well have discarded it as a failed experiment and reverted to orthodox tactics.

In the event, McCabe's innings represented a lone gesture of defiance against a frighteningly effective attack. The Australian batsmen were routed in the second innings, and England won by 10 wickets. Even McCabe would not have looked ahead to the other Tests with confidence, for he knew better than anyone how lucky he had been. He played most of his scoring shots where the Englishmen intended him to play them, on the leg side, but somehow the balls he hit in the air never went to hand. Years later McCabe described his innings as a 'Sydney-or-the-bush' effort. 'I had a charmed life,' he said. 'I was lucky. I could have been out any time.' Luck never allowed him to get on top of bodyline again.

Over the years dozens of cricket books have described McCabe's innings, but here is a first-hand account of it that has never been published before. It is contained in a letter written by Lady Game, the wife of the New South Wales Governor, Sir Philip Game, to her mother in England. After watching McCabe in action, she wrote: 'The last of the Australian team were in and McCabe was batting splendidly for them and kept hitting boundaries and managing extraordinarily cleverly to get the bowling, and though one knows nothing about cricket one admired him very much — he made 180 I think and was cheered to the echo.

'There were I believe 60,000 people there and they really are like children over it — screaming with excitement, yelling, clapping, cheering and almost going off their heads about their own men. It makes one feel that games are a mistake when one sees them behaving like that, and even the Bridges who were with us could hardly contain themselves and Mr Bridge goes so far as to say that Larwood's bowling 'isn't fair', I believe, and he and General Anderson, who is English to the core, could hardly be safely put together. Isn't it silly!'

The second Test was in Melbourne, and Don Bradman was back in the team. A world record crowd of 63,993 turned up on the first day, attracted by the prospect of seeing him deal with England's bodyline bowlers once and for all. He was known to be in form: on the same ground a few days earlier he had made 157 in 199 minutes for New South Wales against Victoria, scoring the last 50 in less than half an hour.

Early in the Australian innings, Bob Wyatt was fielding near the boundary and heard some people shout to him: 'Wait till our Don comes in.' When Bradman did come in he received an ovation which is still remembered by anyone who heard it. The applause rolled on and on like thunder until some time after Bradman had arrived at the crease. Then a momentous anticlimax. Bradman was bowled first ball. He swung mightily at a short delivery from Bill Bowes outside the off stump and dragged it back into his stumps. The crowd was shocked into silence. Bowes could not believe his luck: he had pulled a jackpot with his first coin.

Jardine could not believe his luck, either. Losing control of himself for perhaps the only time that summer, he danced in a circle with his arms above his head — as Bowes says, rather like a Red Indian. Not long ago Bowes demonstrated Jardine's dance for me in the lounge room of his home in Yorkshire. After 50 years, it was still possible to sense Jardine's jubilation that day in Melbourne.

Taking advantage of a fairly docile wicket that took much of the sting out of the English fast bowling, Bradman made 103 not out in the second innings. Bill O'Reilly twice bowled England out cheaply, finishing with 10 wickets for the match, and Australia won the Test by 111 runs.

Gubby Allen remains convinced to this day that it was not until the first innings of the Melbourne Test that bodyline came into being. Before that, he says, England's method of attack was really fast leg theory, admittedly of an aggressive kind. The transition to bodyline (which he defines simply as leg theory with a lot of bouncers) took place, he says, almost by accident.

'Harold busted his boots and he was twice off the field for quite a little time', Allen says. 'The crowd was yelling "Put Larwood on", and the atmosphere was getting pretty tense, not only in the crowd but amongst the players as well. Now back comes Harold and Douglas asked me to tell him to bowl — he wouldn't speak to him. Harold's temper was up a bit, and he rushed in and he started to bowl a lot of bouncers. As he did bowl the bouncers, Douglas moved more fielders on to the legside and brought them up into close-ish positions. It was the first sign of what in my opinion became bodyline.'

I heard elsewhere of Jardine's refusal to speak to Larwood after he returned with his new boots. Apparently, Jardine was annoyed with him for being so long off the field.

It was before play on the first day of the Melbourne Test that Allen was asked by Jardine to bowl what later became known as bodyline and refused to do so. This is the account Allen gave me of the incident.

'Douglas came to me in the dressing room and he said, "I want you to bowl a few more bouncers and have a stronger legside field", or words to that effect. I said, "No Douglas, I never bowl like that and I don't think it's the way the game should be played." He said, "You've got to do it." and I said, "Well, Douglas, I'm not going to and you'll have to make up your mind whether you want me to play or not." I left him but later I said "Am I playing?" and he said, "Of course you're playing. What are you talking about?" and away we went and I bowled just as I always have bowled. He never once tackled me again. To his great credit he accepted my point of view and we remained the best of friends throughout the tour.'

It has never been established exactly which English players were for bodyline and which were against it. Apart from Jardine, the players known to have been for it included the great opening batsman Herbert Sutcliffe (who, incidentally, Australians suspected of being possibly its most ardent supporter), the three fast bowlers who used it, Larwood, Voce and Bowes, and the reserve wicketkeeper George Duckworth. Allen was the only one to object to it openly, but it is likely many of the other English players were passive opponents.

The vice-captain, Bob Wyatt, was certainly one of these. Gubby Allen recalls a conversation he had with Wyatt before the Melbourne Test. 'We were just geting a little suspicious that things were building up and Bob and I discussed it. I said I was dead against any rough stuff and he said so was he. But we decided that while we might discuss it among ourselves we must never at any moment start talking to other members of the team about it and we should never discuss it with anybody in Australia at all. I never, never did.'

Bill Bowes remembers Allen's silent protest. 'When we had team discussions about tactics,' he says, 'Gubby would just keep quiet. He didn't give any dissenting voice or anything — he just kept quiet.'

Allen says he opposed Jardine over bodyline on only one other occasion. 'One day when we were miles away from the cricket ground, I did say, "Oh, Douglas, please try and quieten it down a bit — it really is getting rather awful," and he didn't answer.' Allen says that far from being disloyal to Jardine he was probably Jardine's best friend in Australia. 'He didn't have very many,' he says.

But Jardine had no intention of quietening it down. He knew bodyline had demoralized the Australian batsmen and he was determined to keep up the pressure. In the third Test at Adelaide, bodyline was used more rigorously than ever. Larwood struck the Australian captain Bill Woodfull a terrific blow over the heart and fractured the skull of the Australian wicketkeeper Bert Oldfield. The storms that had been gathering at Sydney and Melbourne had finally broken.

THE BLOW-UP

OF ALL the characters in the bodyline story, none played so intriguing a role as the English team's manager, Pelham Warner. Well-born and genteel of manner, he had come to Australia hoping to spread the idea of cricket's good fellowship, only to find himself dragged into the most bitter controversy in the game's history. It was he, not the English captain, Douglas Jardine, who was rebuked by the Australian captain, Bill Woodfull, when things came to a head in the third Test at Adelaide.

The circumstances could not have been less pleasant. Woodfull had been hit in the chest by Harold Larwood and he was stretched out in the dressing room waiting for a doctor to examine the bruise when Warner came in to express his sympathy. Jack Fingleton was in the dressing room at the time and he later described how Woodfull had at first declined even to speak to Warner, but had then turned to him and said: 'There are two teams out there on the oval. One is playing cricket, the other is not. This game is too good to be spoilt. It is time some people got out of it.'

Warner turned in embarrassment and hurried out of the room. It had been a mortifying experience for him, and there is no doubt he was deeply wounded by it. He must have cursed Jardine silently for bringing the whole nasty business down on their heads.

He even received hate mail in the days that followed. Here is a note sent to him by a Tasmanian man on 19 January: 'Warner, you are a liar of the lowest order. A liar is as low as anyone can go, but a liar who shields himself behind thousands of miles of communications is a liar of liars.' We can imagine how this must have been received by a man of Warner's sensibilities.

The incident in the Australian dressing room was only the start of Warner's troubles. On the same day, Saturday 14 January 1933, Woodfull complained about Jardine's tactics to four members of the Board of Control, the forerunner of the Australian Cricket Board, who were at the Adelaide Oval watching the match. They were B. V. Scrymgour, H. W. Hodgetts and R. F. Middleton of South Australia and Bill Kelly of Victoria. New evidence shows that it was these four men who drafted the famous cable of protest to the MCC in London. They had seen Bill Ponsford hit innumerable times, for he had adopted the novel tactic of simply turning his back into the short-pitched balls. They had seen Don Bradman and Stan McCabe both go out cheaply to Larwood, caught in the bodyline trap.

But what would have dismayed them most was Jardine's decision to move his men into the bodyline cordon almost immediately after Woodfull was hit. Given the likelihood that Woodfull was still feeling groggy, this was a highly intimidating move, which even Jardine came to regret. 'Had either he (Larwood) or I realized the misrepresentation to which we were to be subjected,' Jardine wrote, 'neither of us would have set that field for that particular over.'

It seems the Board's decision to send the cable was prompted by Woodfull's complaint. The Board's secretary, Bill Jeanes, hinted at this in a cable he sent to a Board member a few days later. 'Mr Woodfull complained to Mr Warner about the tactics adopted by the MCC team and to members of the Board and to myself,' Jeanes said. 'He expressed the opinion that the Board should take prompt action in the matter.' However, the idea of the cable may actually have been conceived by the Board's chairman, Dr Allan Robertson, who was in Melbourne but was consulted by phone by the four Board members in Adelaide. In correspondence written at the time, Jeanes spoke of the four men 'concurring' with a suggestion that a cable be sent, which indicates the suggestion came from someone else. This could only have been Dr Robertson.

We now know that the Board's decision to send the cable was by no means unanimous. Eight Board members voted for it and five against. (The eight in favour were from Victoria, South Australia, Tasmania and Western Australia, and the five against were from New South Wales and Victoria. The two Queensland members expressed the view that the Board should not have acted without receiving a specific complaint in writing from Woodfull.) The cable was sent at 3.12 pm on 18 January, the day before England won the Test. It said:

'Bodyline bowling assumed such proportions as to menace best interests of the game, making protection of body by batsmen the main consideration and causing intensely bitter feelings amongst players as well as injury. In our opinion it is unsportsmanlike and unless stopped at once it is likely to upset friendly relations existing between Australia and England.'

Bodyline had now moved from controversy to crisis. Conservative newspapers such as *The Sydney Morning Herald,* which had written editorials defending bodyline after the first Test, were now writing editorials denouncing it. A Sydney district court judge, John Sheridan, went so far as to warn that although the laws of cricket did not prohibit bodyline the *Crimes Act* did. Judge Sheridan said: 'I gather that people contend that though body bowling is dangerous it is not prohibited by the rules of cricket. I would suggest that it may be covered by the criminal law. By our *Crimes Act* it is a serious offence maliciously to wound a man or inflict grievous bodily harm upon him, and to quote Section 5 of that Act: "Every act done without malice but with reckless indifference to human life or suffering . . . shall be taken to have been done maliciously within the meaning of this Act".'

Even Jardine was worried. The abuse he was subjected to by the Adelaide crowd did not bother him: on the contrary, he seemed to goad the crowd into abusing him more. He called a meeting of his players to make sure they were behind him, and found they were. But as Gubby Allen recalls today, Jardine had one fear — that the MCC would not support him.

Allen says: 'I remember Douglas saying to me, "Have you seen the cable?" And I said, "Yes I have — it's awful". He said, "That word unsportsmanlike . . ." I said, "Douglas, you're absolutely wrong. That's the best thing that could have happened." He said, "No, they'll let me down at Lord's." And I said, "Douglas, no one can call an Englishman unsporting and get away with it. They'll back you to the hilt." I can still see the smile that came over his face. He thought I'd perhaps hit the nail on the head.'

And so it proved. In its reply on 24 January, the MCC deplored the Board's cable, including in particular the word 'unsportsmanlike' professed faith in Jardine and said it was ready to call off the rest of the tour.

Poor Warner. He had tried to stop the row spreading beyond Adelaide and now it had become an international issue. But the MCC had spoken, and he thought that would be the end of the matter.

On 31 January the Board sent its second cable to the MCC. It was phrased more tactfully than the first, but it did not retract the word 'unsportsmanlike' and it asserted that bodyline was 'opposed to the spirit of cricket and dangerous to the players'. Whether because of some secret message he received from the MCC or, more probably, because of the refusal by Jardine to captain England in the fourth Test unless a full retraction was made. Warner suddenly became afraid the rest of the tour would be cancelled.

Some leverage was obviously needed to make the Board back down, and Warner appealed for help to the one man who could arrange it. By doing so, he must have realized he was elevating a controversy over cricket into the region of high politics. On 1 February he and his co-manager, Palairet, sent the following telegram to the British Government's representative in Australia, Ernest Crutchley. 'Have under consideration cancellation of remaining matches of tour including Test owing to failure of board to withdraw stigma of word unsportsmanlike in their first cable. Beg you use your influence to get word withdrawn. Matter very urgent.'

There followed then a remarkable intervention in the affair by the Prime Minister, Joseph Lyons. Lyons was both an Anglophile and a cricket enthusiast, so he would have been well disposed to helping out. But still it is intriguing that he was prepared to get involved.

He did so, apparently without hesitation, when Crutchley phoned him on 1 February and asked for help. From a cable that recently came to light in Melbourne we know what action Lyons took. The cable was sent by Dr Robertson to the Board's secretary, Jeanes, on the same day, 1 February. It said: 'Prime Minister interviewed me today. Stated that British representative had seen him and asked him to get us to withdraw word objected to. If not likelihood of England pulling right out. If we do withdraw has no doubt [English bowling] attack will be modified. Government afraid successful conversions endangered.'

This contains the startling disclosure that the Australian Government feared its 'conversions,' meaning conversion loans from Britain, had been placed at risk by the bodyline row. These conversion loans — actually old loans

renegotiated, or converted, to allow easier repayment — were of crucial importance to the capital-starved Australian economy during the Depression. Any interference with them could have had disastrous consequences.

Assuming Lyons did not just pretend to be worried about them to put pressure on the Board, what, or who, was the cause of his concern? Did Crutchley hint that the bad feeling over the cricket was alienating British financiers? Or did Lyons receive a warning about the loans from within his Government, perhaps originating at Australia House in London? After all, he did tell Robertson that it was the Government, not he personally, who was worried.

The answers to these questions might well have been found in a file opened at the time by the Prime Minister's Department under the heading English Cricket Team 1932. The file's catalogue number was 748/1/291. Unfortunately, the file has disappeared, without trace and without explanation.

Both Lyons and Crutchley tried to conceal their involvement in the affair. Speaking in Newcastle a month later, Lyons said it had been suggested to him at the start of the summer that he would find relief from the cares of his duties by following the Tests, for cricket was one matter at least that he did not have to give official attention to. Now, he had found himself being phoned at night by some newspaper reporter asking if it were true that he had been conferring with a British Government representative about bodyline bowling. The audience laughed, no doubt thinking the idea a preposterous one. Lyons probably laughed to himself, too, knowing it was all completely true. According to Lyons, incidentally, the rumours about his involvement had originated in London. Obviously, Crutchley had reported to Whitehall on his dealings with Lyons, and word of it had somehow got about there. After the rumour was denied, it seems to have had no further currency.

Crutchley said nothing about his part in the affair until the story was confirmed elsewhere. Then, on 3 February, he issued a statement in which he said ... 'Both managers (Warner and Palairet) are very good friends of mine and I know how they are feeling about the stigma which they attach to the use of that word (unsportsmanlike). I feel that anything that might interfere with the continuation of the tour, or even prevent the rest of the tour being carried out in an atmosphere of complete friendship and harmony, would be a calamity, so I did what I could to help.' However, he never revealed that he had actually been in touch with the Australian Prime Minister. It may be noted that Warner and Palairet were strongly criticized in some quarters in Australia for bringing Crutchley into it. It was an insult to the Board of Control according to one New South Wales cricket official, J. D. Durham, who said: 'It appears to me the English managers are making an attempt to force the hand of the Board.' This was certainly true.

There was other activity at the political level. The Governor of South Australia, Sir Alexander Hore-Ruthven, was on leave in England, but the Acting Governor, Sir George Murray, invited Pelham Warner and a number of prominent Adelaide citizens to Government House to discuss the matter. One man at the meeting, Lloyd Dumas, the editor of *The Advertiser* newspaper, wrote later that Warner was 'emphatic in his condemnation of what was being done, but, on the field, Jardine was in complete control'.

The upshot of the meeting was that a report was sent to Hore-Ruthven in London. Apparently alarmed by its contents, Hore-Ruthven immediately took the matter to the highest level. On 31 January he called on the British Cabinet minister responsible for the Dominions, Jimmy Thomas. According to the Australian Press Association at the time, it was as a direct result of Hore-Ruthven's visit that Thomas met MCC committee members at his office on the following day, 1 February. Hore-Ruthven was also present at that meeting, but all he would tell a reporter about it afterwards was: 'My part in the negotiations was purely personal and informal, due to a desire to help in smoothing out the cricket troubles. I prefer to say nothing more about it.'

Lyon's intervention proved successful. Exactly a week after he had got in touch with the Board, the Board sent another cable to the MCC which began: 'We do not regard the sportsmanship of your team as being in question ...' The crisis was at once defused and the British loans, presumably, were out of danger. But the withdrawal had been embarrassing for the Board.

The Board's retraction came just in time. It was cabled on February 8, two days before the fourth Test was due to start in Brisbane, so the Test was able to go ahead as scheduled. Jardine had made it clear that, irrespective of what the rest of his team did, he would not captain England in another Test until the retraction was made. When he heard of the Board's cable, he made a 12-minute radio-telephone call to London, the purpose of which was not revealed.

THE ASHES WON

AFTER the sensations at Adelaide, the last two Tests, at Brisbane and Sydney, seemed rather an anticlimax. England won both of them, which meant it regained the Ashes by the overwhelming margin of four Tests to one. It was a result made possible by Jardine's achievement of the seemingly impossible: he had subdued Don Bradman.

At Brisbane, the Australians had their best start of the series, ending the first day at 3 for 251. Woodfull and Richardson made an opening partnership of 133, and at stumps Bradman was 71 not out. *The Sydney Morning Herald* was bold enough to say in a heading, 'Leg Theory Mastered', but it spoke far too soon. On the following day Larwood bowled Bradman almost immediately, and the last seven Australian wickets fell for only 89 runs. In its second innings Australia was shot out for just 175. It was a commendable performance by the English bowlers, particularly in view of Voce's absence from the side.

The last Test at Sydney followed a similar pattern — Australia did well in the first innings, scoring 435, but could manage only 182 in the second. For Larwood, it was a match of mixed fortunes. He made 98 and took four wickets in Australia's first innings, but broke down with a fractured toe in the second. The story has often been told of how Jardine made Larwood stay on the field until Bradman was out, with the result that the two men walked off the field together. Hammond made the winning run for England with a huge off-drive for six into the Sheridan Stand. There were few people who were not immensely relieved it was all over.

Bradman's batting throughout the series was audacious to an astonishing degree. Newspaper reports tell us that some of his shots were so unorthodox they made the crowd gasp. Jack Fingleton called it 'Alice-in-Wonderland' batting, and a typical example of it was cutting Larwood off his leg stump. 'Only a batsman with phenomenal sight and footwork could do that,' Larwood wrote in his book, *The Larwood Story*.

I have heard from someone who watched the fifth Test at Sydney and still thrills at the memory of Bradman tennis-smashing a bouncer from Larwood straight back over the bowler's head with such force that it struck the sightscreen on the first bounce.

Bradman's policy seemed to be to score as many runs as he could while his luck held out. This is illustrated by the fact that he made his runs in the Tests at an average rate of 4·5 for each six balls faced, which would be reckoned a brisk rate today even in one-day cricket. Several times he seemed to have bodyline beaten, but lost his wicket before he had built up a big score. He was hit only once — by Larwood in the fifth Test. It bruised his left arm and he could not field on the following day.

His scores in the Tests were: 0, 103 not out, 8, 66, 76, 24, 48 and 71. Although his average for the series, 56·6, was only half as high as it might otherwise have been, it was much higher than the average of any other Australian and higher than the average of any English batsman except Eddie Paynter, who played in only three Tests and was dismissed only three times.

John Arlott recalls a conversation he had with Jardine about the bodyline tour many years later. 'You know, we nearly didn't do it,' Jardine said. 'The little man was bloody good.' It was probably the nicest thing Jardine ever said about Don Bradman.

THE AFTERMATH

DOUGLAS Jardine in his later years did not talk much about the bodyline affair, but when he did it was never with regret. To the end, his victory over the Australians in 1932–33 gave him deep satisfaction. John Arlott remembers him, long after the war, rubbing his hands and recalling with triumph, 'We did it, we did it.'

What he and his men did, of course, was to stifle Don Bradman's scoring and regain the Ashes. But England did not thank him for long. Soon after his team returned to England, the MCC began to swing around to the view that bodyline was unfair. In 1934 it banned bodyline, in effect, by prohibiting any direct attack by a bowler on a batsman.

Aware of the changing mood at Lord's, Jardine declined to play against the Australians who came to England in 1934 and later that year he retired from first-class cricket altogether. Jardine felt he had been betrayed by the MCC. His daughter, Mrs Fianach Lawry, says: 'My mother used to say he was bitter about it. There were painful memories.' Jardine's widow, incidentally, now lives in Malta.

Harold Larwood, too, refused to play against the Australians in 1934. It had been suggested to him that he ought to apologize to the MCC for bowling bodyline in Australia if he wanted to be chosen for the Tests. Larwood refused to do this and announced in an article that he would never play against the Australians again. He never did, although he continued playing for Nottinghamshire until 1938. He has made no secret of the fact that, in his opinion, the MCC made him a scapegoat.

There is in existence some fascinating correspondence between the Board of Control and its representative in England, Dr Robert Macdonald, a former Queensland cricketer, in 1933 and 1934. It reveals that the Board put pressure on the MCC to dump Jardine.

In a letter to the Board on 2 January 1934, Macdonald said he had told the MCC that in 1934 'there would be an immediate and complete restoration of those amicable relations which, previous to Jardine, had always marked the great Test matches between England and Australia; but that if Jardine was made captain in 1934 the contest would not be England versus Australia or Australia versus England but Jardine versus Australia and Australia versus Jardine, and that under his captaincy there would be a veiled vendetta.'

Macdonald seems to have detested Jardine. In the same letter to the Board, he said: 'Australia will have the satisfaction of knowing that she resented the introduction into

cricket of methods which (while quite natural to Mr Jardine) were wholly Teutonic in character. To achieve victory at any cost seems to be an attribute common to both Attila and Mr Jardine. If I do Attila an injustice by this simile I tender an apology to his belated memory.'

Macdonald warned the Board, given the delicacy of the situation, to choose its words carefully when dealing with the MCC. This applied even to how it referred to bodyline bowling. 'I have always referred to it as "that type of bowling in Australia to which exception was taken by Australia",' Macdonald wrote on 7 August 1933. 'I think it would be safer for you to use that description of it when you cable the MCC.'

'If we used the term bodyline it would arouse resentment here: if we used the term leg-theory (the MCC appellation) it would to our Australian minds not be a true definition of Jardine's methods. I would advise you when cabling to the MCC to use very friendly language for at this particular moment it will materially help our cause.'

Macdonald's biggest problem was that people in England, including the top people in the MCC, were largely ignorant of the kind of tactics Jardine had used in Australia. This state of affairs has usually been blamed on the weakness of the English press contingent which followed the tour, but Macdonald also believed that British newspapers had virtually censored stories critical of Jardine.

For instance, as he told the Board in a letter in June 1933, it had never been reported in England that Jardine moved his men into the bodyline trap after Bill Woodfull had been hit by Larwood in the Adelaide Test, even though this action by Jardine had been more widely condemned in Australia than any other. In a conversation, a month earlier, with the secretary of the MCC, Billy Findlay, Macdonald had discovered even he was not aware of it. 'If that incident at Adelaide had been published here, Jardine's mentality and ruthlessness would have been markedly revealed to the English people. The veil of silence was drawn over it by the English press.'

Gubby Allen remembers encountering the same kind of ignorance when he returned to England and met Billy Findlay at Lord's. Findlay said to him: 'What a terrible time you must have had in Australia ... I refuse to believe that any Englishman ever bowled at a batsman.' Allen replied: 'The sooner you try to find out what's been going on, the better for cricket.' As a result of that exchange, Findlay and Allen did not speak to each other for two years.

The bodyline furore had some unexpected repercussions. In a letter to the British Dominions Secretary, Jimmy Thomas, in June 1933, the Governor of South Australia, Sir Alexander Hore-Ruthven, spoke of the ill-feeling it had produced and said: 'That feeling rankles even to the extent of reluctance to buy English goods, which businessmen inform me is going on to a certain extent in this city today.' It was also reported that sales of Australian wine had declined in England.

Even more remarkable was the following report from an Australian journalist in the Far East named J. S. Hughes, who said that even the *North China Daily News* had taken a pro-bodyline stance. 'It was remarkable', he wrote, 'how the bodyline business had militated against Australia in certain quarters of the Far East. It was impossible not to be struck by the heat it had engendered and by its bad effect on our commercial interests in China. This may seem rather far-fetched, but is nevertheless a fact that Australians engaged in business in Hong Kong and Shanghai have been embarrassed by it. I know of several deals lost to Australians because of it.'

A REFLECTION

LARWOOD appears to be the only survivor of Jardine's team who remains entirely unrepentant about bodyline. Bowes still thinks bodyline was fair, but he admits it may have had to be banned because of its danger to batsmen. Even Bill Voce, according to one of his team-mates, has come to believe bodyline was bad for the game. This could not be confirmed, because Voce refused to discuss anything connected with bodyline. 'I'm fed up with it,' he said. 'I'm not having any more.'

All the survivors of Jardine's team, including one or two who disliked Jardine personally and objected to his tactics, have remained remarkably loyal to him. None has forgotten his indomitable spirit in Australia when he braved the rage of a whole nation. Bill Bowes says simply, 'He was probably the greatest man I ever knew.'

Gubby Allen says: 'I'm sorry he didn't try and quieten it down a bit. I think he let it get a little bit too rough. On some occasions Douglas could be exceedingly difficult — I don't think anybody denies that — but that he was in any way a rogue, I would never agree.'

After 50 years' musing about bodyline, some of the surviving players have made interesting conclusions about the reasons for its success. Gubby Allen, for instance, believes that the variable bounce of the Australian wickets that summer was a key factor, the importance of which has never been appreciated. 'Harold would rush in, drop one a bit short and it would come through, say, shoulder high. The next one would drop in exactly the same spot and come through hip high. The number of times I saw that happen ... Now, the Australians used to go and duck — there are millions of pictures of them doing it, ducking and getting hit. Or if a ball came through hip high they would decide to stand up and play the next one, and it would come through shoulder high. It made it very, very difficult.

'I think bodyline would have succeeded in any case, but it would never have had anything like the success and, indeed, the number of people being hit, if it had not been this uneven bounce.'

Nobody has thought of a sure counter to bodyline. English players who have pondered the problem, including Allen and Bob Wyatt, think the Australians might have fared better if they had taken guard outside the leg stump. Their theory is that a batsman taking normal guard had two things to worry about when a ball bounced in his direction: would it hit him or would it hit the stumps? If it bounced at him when he took guard outside the leg stump, he had only one thing to worry about: getting out of its way.

Bill Bowes says his great regret about bodyline was that Bradman did not try harder to find a means of combatting it. 'There may not have been an answer to it,' he says, 'but if there was, Bradman was the one man who could have come up with it. But he damned it as soon as he saw it. I will always be sorry he did not really give it a go.'

Bradman, of course, long outlasted the bodyline controversy. Seventeen months after Jardine's men won the last Test in Australia, Bradman scored 304 in a Test against England. In the following Test he scored 244. It was almost as though bodyline had never happened. When nearly every member of Jardine's team was retired or dead, Bradman was still scoring Test centuries.

And what of Jardine himself? There is no doubt he mellowed with age. Australians such as Bill O'Reilly and Keith Miller who met him after the war found him charming in the extreme. He acquired business interests in Australia and visited the country in the early 1950s. 'I would like to go out to the Sydney Cricket Ground again,' he told a reporter then. 'I would like to sit on the Hill.'

His daughter, Mrs Fianach Lawry, recalls an incident about 1950 which suggests Jardine continued to take his cricket seriously. She and her sister were playing in a girls' cricket match at their boarding school, and Jardine came along to watch them. Within a few minutes, however, both Jardine girls had been dismissed for low scores. On seeing this their father said, 'Jesus wept!' and turned away in disgust. 'We were left with a sense of completely letting him down,' Mrs Lawry says.

Late in 1957 Jardine took one of his daughters on a trip to Rhodesia, where he owned some land. He developed tick fever there, and when it had not cleared up after his return to England he entered hospital for treatment. The doctors cleared up his tick fever, but they discovered Jardine had lung cancer. He had hardly ever been sick before, and he was only a light smoker. When he started to have trouble breathing, he was sent to a sanatorium in Switzerland, and he died there in June 1958, aged 57.

Jack Fingleton, woken at 3 am in Australia to be told of the news, wrote a marvellous obituary in the *London Daily Express*. 'Not even his bitterest opponent could take from Jardine the greatest tribute of all — he was a man's man.' Fingleton said. 'He saw to it that Bradman was drubbed ... Where I think Jardine made his mistake was in thinking that the Australian eleven was made up of 11 Bradmans.'

Don Bradman in the heyday of his youth.
It is hard to think of another international sportsman,
in any sport, who has established
such a wide margin of supremacy
as Bradman did over the men he played with and against.
His appeal to spectators was tremendous,
and nobody has captured the essence of it better
than the English historian, H. S. Altham.
'In the many pictures that I have stored in my mind from
the "burnt-out Junes" of forty years,'
Altham wrote, 'there is none more dramatic or compelling than that of Bradman's small,
serenely-moving figure in its big-peaked green cap
coming out of the pavilion shadows into the sunshine,
with the concentration, ardour and apprehension
of surrounding thousands centred upon him,
and the destiny of a Test match in his hands.'

Don Bradman, aged 16, at his home at Bowral. He played his first cricket match at the age of 11, made his first century (for Bowral High School against Mittagong High School) when he was 12 and played his first match for the men's team at Bowral when he was 13. A natural sportsman, he was an under-age sprinting champion at school (W.G. Grace, incidentally, was also an outstanding runner in his youth) and was so brilliant at tennis that he was reckoned by some to have a big future in the sport. But cricket was always his first love, and at the age of 17 he began to produce the prodigious feats of batsmanship which a few years later were to amaze the whole cricket world. Playing for Bowral against teams from neighbouring towns, Bradman made scores of 234 and 300 in the summer of 1925–26. The innings of 234 was made against Wingello, whose star bowler was Bill O'Reilly, later to become Australia's premier bowler. Although O'Reilly, then aged nearly 20, eventually bowled Bradman, he was so dispirited by being thrashed by a 17-year-old youth that he felt like giving the game up. 'Little did I realize at the time,' he recalls today, 'that I was just the first cab off the rank.' Bradman's huge scores in the country brought him to the attention of New South Wales' selectors the following summer and in the summer after that, 1927–28, he made his debut in first-class cricket, scoring 118 for New South Wales against South Australia. In an extraordinarily successful career that was to last another 20 years, Bradman experienced only one major setback — when he encountered Jardine's bodyline bowlers in 1932–33.

The Bradman stance, 1930.
Apart from the peculiarity of his grip
and the fact that he rested his bat in front of,
rather than behind, his back foot,
Bradman differed from most other batsmen in that
he remained perfectly still while waiting for the ball.
His bat did not tap and his feet did not shuffle.
He seems to have had the same kind of control over himself off the field.
The English journalist William Pollock wrote in 1933:
'One thing I have noticed is that he can sit still.'

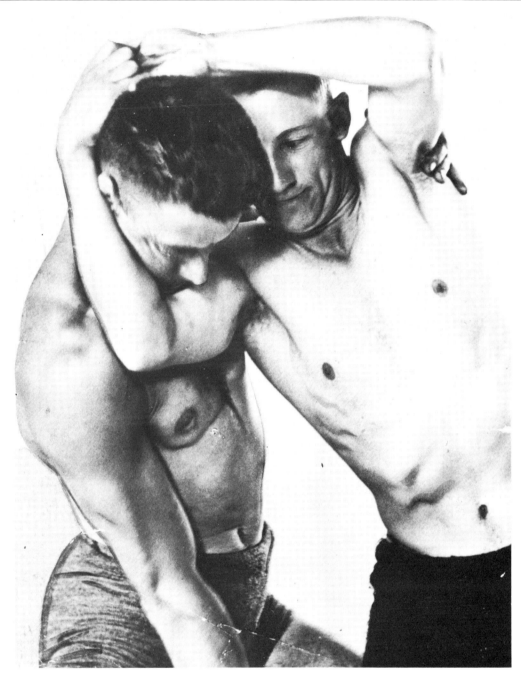

No explanation can be offered for how Don Bradman came to be photographed
demonstrating a wrestling hold,
but this photograph does have the distinction of being apparently
the only one published of Bradman stripped to the waist.
It shows that while he may have been slim he was by no means slight.
He was, in fact, comparatively wide across the chest,
and Pelham Warner once cited physical strength as one of the secrets of his success.
Warner described him as 'short in height, though long in the leg,
and with very broad shoulders'.
Bradman's exact height has not been recorded.
Irving Rosenwater includes an interesting note on the subject in his biography of Bradman.
Although Bradman's height has sometimes been given as 5 feet 8 inches,
Rosenwater observes that the cricket writer Ray Robinson, a reliable judge is most
matters, always said it was actually 5 feet 6¾ inches.
Robinson came to this conclusion, apparently, by comparing Bradman with other
cricketers whose height was known.
For instance, Stan McCabe was 5 feet 8 inches tall, and Bradman was shorter than him.
In summary, it may be said that Bradman was certainly looked upon as a short man,
rather than simply a man of less than medium height.

A group of Queensland players carry 21-year-old Don Bradman
off the Sydney Cricket Ground after he had broken the world record
by scoring 452 not out for New South Wales against Queensland
in January 1930.
It was this innings which really made Bradman a national idol in Australia,
even to the extent that people began writing poems about him.
Bradman made his runs in the extraordinary time of 415 minutes,
displaying the same total mastery over the Queensland bowling which he was to
achieve over the best bowlers in England four months later.

The Bradman smile was an expression of his tremendous self-confidence.
Arthur Mailey wrote in 1932:
'Woodfull's confidence is of a modest nature,
while Bradman's confidence annoys and irritates a bowler.
He is what might be called arrogantly confident.'

Percy Fender.

Jardine as a small boy — wearing a kilt as any Scots boy might have expected to.
This picture was kindly provided by Jardine's daughter, Mrs Lawry.

For a man so fearless in most ways, Jardine was an unusually nervous batsman. This was particularly so while he was waiting to go in. He batted at number 6 in the first two Tests and, according to Bob Wyatt, was a 'bundle of nerves' until it was his turn to bat. After Wyatt, an opener, was out in the first Test at Sydney, he returned to find Jardine sitting behind a post where he couldn't see the game. 'I sat down next to him,' Wyatt says. 'I said, "A beautiful wicket — we'll make 500." He said, "You must be bloody crazy." He was so worked up that he'd got himself into a state.' It was because of his nervousness that the English selection committee decided that Jardine should open the batting, which he did for the last three Tests. The idea was to spare him the anxiety of waiting with his pads on.

The English team in which Jardine made his
first visit to Australia in 1928–29.
Members of this team who toured under Jardine in 1932–33 are:
front row — Duckworth (far left), Ames (next to him) and Tate (second from right);
second row — Leyland (far left),
Hammond (third from left), Sutcliffe (third from right) and Larwood (next to him);
front row — Jardine himself
(second from right).
(A Fishwick Photo)

Hunter Hendry, who had an angry exchange with Jardine
during the latter's first visit to Australia in 1928–29.
Hendry has cause for another reason to remember his encounter with the Englishmen
that summer with mixed feelings — Larwood bowled a kind of bodyline at him.
It was during the second Test at Sydney, when Hendry and Woodfull
were both in the process of making centuries.
Apparently in desperation, Larwood used a form of attack which closely approximated
what four years later came to be known as bodyline.
However, he used it only briefly and without success,
and its significance was not appreciated at the time.
This is how one newspaper described it:
'Undoubtedly the English bowling was mastered.
Larwood was forced to change his tactics.
At one stage he adopted a short-leg theory field,
pitching his deliveries short and bumping them at the batsmen.
He did not succeed,
and later reverted to the orthodox deployment.'

Hunter Hendry shows his disappointment at being ruled leg-before to Larwood in the first Test in 1928–29 by looking pointedly at the position of his left leg. To this day he insists he was trying to leg glance a ball several inches outside his leg stump when he was hit on the pad. Hendry believes some of the English players had berated the umpire for disallowing an appeal for a catch behind against him towards the end of the previous day's play and that the umpire was therefore under pressure to uphold the next confident appeal. The other batsman is Jack Ryder. This Test was Don Bradman's first.

Douglas Jardine at home. If it still existed, the Harlequin cap that he wore which so irritated Australian crowds would be prized by any cricket museum. According to his daughter, Mrs Lawry, however, the cap became moth-eaten and, after Jardine's death, his wife burnt it. This picture is from Mrs Lawry's collection.

'I am sorry to disappoint anyone', Jardine wrote, 'who has imagined that the leg theory was evolved with the help of midnight oil and iced towels, simply and solely for the purpose of combating Bradman's effectiveness as a scoring machine. However highly Bradman may have been rated, this view was exaggerated.' In fact, all the evidence suggests that this view was not exaggerated at all. There does not seem to be one survivor of Jardine's team today who does not believe that bodyline was developed specifically to curb Bradman's scoring. It is safe to say that if there had been no Bradman there would have been no bodyline.

At the time of the 1932–33 tour, Jardine must have been considered a highly eligible bachelor. He was 32 years old, distinguished in manner and appearance and known to be well off. Wyatt says he had a few girlfriends in Australia, and there is other evidence to show that he certainly had a girlfriend in Sydney. 'But he wasn't any kind of playboy or lady-killer,' Wyatt says.

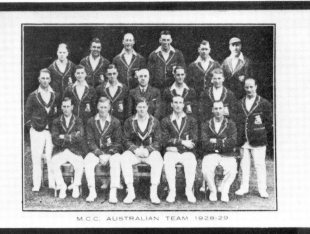

Christmas greetings sent from Jardine during his first tour to Australia in 1928–29.

Ponsford in his prime, batting against the Englishmen in 1928–29.
(A Fishwick Photo.)

Bert Oldfield was Australia's wicketkeeper for
almost the whole period between the wars,
having risen to prominence in the illustrious AIF
team during World War I. Bob Wyatt says that
the two Australian players Jardine liked most
were Oldfield and Vic Richardson.

(A Fishwick photo)

Bill Woodfull had more trouble handling bodyline than some of the other Australians because he was not quick on his feet. However, as Bill O'Reilly recalls, he was always ready to move down the pitch to play the slow bowlers. He demonstrates this here as he hits Arthur Mailey for four in a Sheffield Shield match between Victoria and New South Wales in January 1926. Bert Oldfield is the wicketkeeper and Jack Gregory is in slips.

Clarrie Grimmett — arriving for another match.

Bradman's ability was admired not least by the men who bowled bodyline at him. These are a few of their recorded comments. Larwood: 'Nobody watching the "pat-ball" batsmen of today can have any idea of what Don was like. Good length stuff went to the boundary like a bullet. He used all the shots in the book, and a few that weren't ... "Plum" Warner told reporters privately that Don was the only batsman he had seen who could square cut me from right over the stumps.' Bowes: 'In his early days, if you moved a fieldsman from, say, slips to cover point, spent a long time over it and appeared to be meticulous about getting the man in the exact position, while all the time assuming an I'll-get-you-out-now attitude, you could bet Don would rise to the bait. Your next ball would be cracked like a bullet past the cover-point fieldsman, or he would cut it through a gap in the slips ... The crowd roared with glee. You have been made to look a fool.' Voce (when asked by Neville Cardus what was the best ball to bowl at Bradman): 'There's no ruddy best ball to bowl at the Don.'

These pictures of Larwood are from film footage in the possession of The *Age* in Melbourne. The film was apparently shot in England, although whether in a genuine match (the umpire seems to be looking at Larwood's foot closely enough) it cannot now be said. Larwood is obviously not extending himself in this delivery, but the grace and power of his action are still apparent. Jack Egan of Sydney recently made a television documentary on cricket, in which Larwood and Ray Lindwall are shown, on separate halves of the screen, running in to bowl. The two men seem almost to be synchronized, so closely do they resemble each other in their approach to the wicket and their bowling action. This is no accident: as an 11-year-old boy Lindwall watched closely while Harold Larwood was bowling at the Sydney Cricket Ground in 1932–33.

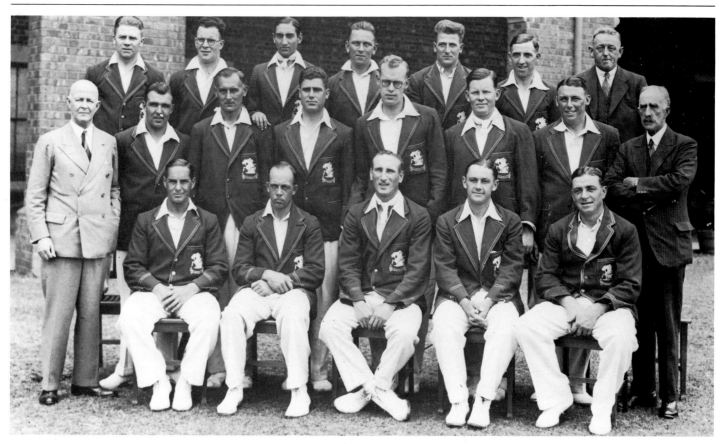

The touring side. Top row – Duckworth, Mitchell, Pataudi, Leyland,
Larwood, Paynter, Bill Ferguson (scorer and baggage man).
Second row — Pelham Warner (co-manager), Ames, Verity, Voce, Bowes, Brown, Tate,
R. C. N. Palairet (co-manager).
Bottom row — Sutcliffe, Wyatt, Jardine, Allen, Hammond. (A Fishwick Photo)

Sir Otto Niemeyer, the British financier, at a conference in Australia in 1930.
When Australia became stricken by the Depression and doubts arose about its
ability to repay loans from Britain, the Bank of England sent Niemeyer to
Australia to safeguard its interests. Niemeyer's prescription for Australia, a big
cut in wages, made him highly unpopular with ordinary Australians. It is said
that Australians were afterwards inclined to blame the British ruling class, as
represented by Niemeyer, for much of the misery they suffered during the
Depression. It has even been speculated that many Australians felt an instinctive
antipathy towards Jardine because he seemed, by his manner and appearance, to
belong to that same ruling class.

Don Bradman and his wife Jessie, a friend since childhood, in November 1932. They had married earlier that year.

Cheerful and already suntanned, Jardine arrives at Fremantle on 18 October 1932.

Kangaroo : *"Welcome and good luck, Leo."*

Leo : *"Thanks—er" (hastily)—"what's the latest about Bradman?"*

This cartoon, which appeared after the arrival of the English team at Perth, was quite correct in suggesting that the Englishmen were preoccupied with the threat that Bradman presented to them. The book in the lion's pocket is titled, rather ominously, *How to Get Bradman Out.*

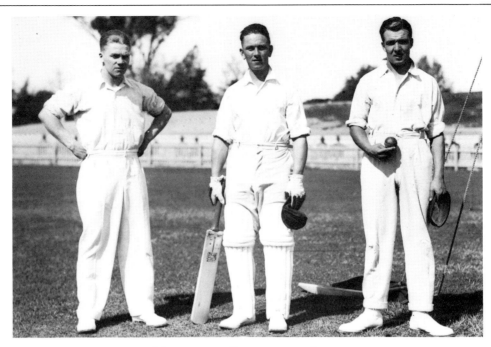

Duckworth, **L**eyland and **A**mes.

Duckworth (left) and Allen on the liner Orontes which brought them to Australia.
Duckworth had kept wickets for England in the Tests of 1930, and one story has it that
it was he who first noticed that Bradman was uneasy against
Larwood's lifting deliveries at the Oval that year.
Several English players have said that it was Bradman's uncertainty
that day which encouraged Jardine to use bodyline against him two years later.
Bradman, however, has strongly disputed this.

Jardine in the nets at Perth at the start of the tour,
October 1932.

Watched by bare-footed boys, Pelham ('Plum') Warner, the more senior of the
two English managers, gives the English players fielding practice at Perth soon
after their arrival in Australia. Warner, who turned 59 at the start of the tour,
had been to Australia twice before. He captained the English teams which toured
in 1903–04 and 1911–12. Like Jardine, Warner was both a lawyer and an Oxford
graduate. The cap he is wearing here, the multi-coloured Harlequin cap, was
awarded to him for playing cricket for Oxford. Jardine wore the same kind of
cap for the same reason — much to the irritation of Australian crowds. Warner
was knighted in 1937 and was later president of the MCC.

This is how Bill Bowes recalls his celebrated row with Jardine after the English captain wanted to set a legside field for him, in the second match of the tour at Adelaide, without explaining the purpose for it: 'Vic Richardson was batting — he pulled the ball very well, you know — and I bowled a bouncer and Vic pulled it, so I asked for a man over. Jardine said, "You can't have one." So I bowled another bouncer which Vic Richardson pulled, but I still didn't have a man over. So I bowled another bouncer again — this went on and I asked again for a man over. Jardine said, "No, but you can have three." I said, "Why three?" He had no reply: he walked away. So I bowled short until I was taken off. Jardine said afterwards, "I want to have a word with you." I said, "Yes, and I want to have a word with you, skipper." Then, going back to the hotel he said, "Look, if you don't do as I tell you I'll send you home." So I said, "I'll go. I'll go tomorrow if you say so." He said, "Do you mean that?" I said, "Yes. I can't bowl just as you say if you don't tell me what your ideas are." And then he said he had this idea for leg-theory. It was the first time I'd heard about it.'

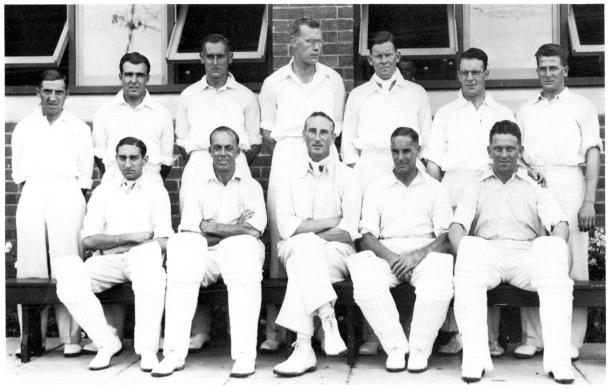

The team that played the opening match of the tour
— against Western Australia at Perth. Back row — Paynter, Ames, Verity, Bowes,
Brown, Mitchell, Larwood.
Front row — Pataudi, Wyatt, Jardine, Sutcliffe, Leyland.

Gubby Allen practising. So much public attention has been concentrated on Larwood's great speed in 1932–33 that it tends to be forgotten that Allen, too, bowled at a very lively pace. Larwood himself insists that Allen bowled faster than he did against the Australians in 1930. Allen took 21 wickets in the bodyline Tests — second only to Larwood, who took 33. If he had bowled bodyline as Jardine wanted him to, he no doubt would have taken more wickets and the Australians would have found their task even more difficult.

Victor Richardson, captain of South Australia and the grandfather of the Chappell brothers. He was a strong hooker of the ball, but he had little success against the short-pitched bowling of Larwood and Voce in 1932–33. According to the Australian journalist R. W. E. Wilmot, Richardson 'stood straight up to it'. Wilmot wrote: 'He watched the ball carefully, and swayed his body to left or right in order to avoid it, and was seldom hit.' Richardson was one of the few, perhaps the only, Australian batsman who tried to counter bodyline by taking guard outside the leg stump — a tactic which some of the Englishmen, including Allen and Wyatt, believed to be well worth trying.

The English party photographed during their first visit to Adelaide with the South Australian Governor, Sir Alexander Hore-Ruthven, and several Australian players, past and present. From left, they are: (back row) — Allen, Bill Jeanes (the Board of Control's secretary), Duckworth, Palairet (the team's co-manager), Ames, Larwood, Verity, Bowes, Brown, Voce, Vic Richardson (captain of South Australia), Pataudi, Clarrie Grimmett (the Australian bowler), Jack Hobbs (who came on the tour as a cricket writer), Leyland and Legh Winser (the Governor's private secretary); (front row) — unknown, Sutcliffe, Wyatt, unknown, Jardine, Sir Alexander Hore-Ruthven, Warner, Clem Hill (a former Australian captain) and Hammond; (seated in front) — Arthur Mailey (the former Australian spin bowler, who covered the series for a Sydney newspaper), Mitchell and Paynter. Sir Alexander Hore-Ruthven and his secretary, Legh Winser, later played an active part in diplomatic moves to restore good Anglo-Australian relations after the bodyline row blew up.

Bill Voce of Nottinghamshire. An aggressive bowler, he was also regarded by the Australians as rather hot-headed.

As in 1928–29, Jardine (left) was quickly singled out for abuse by the Australian crowds in 1932–33 — even before bodyline had become an issue. He was barracked so much during the second match of the tour at Adelaide (where he scored 108 not out) that Pelham Warner made a special appeal for better crowd behaviour when the Englishmen arrived in the next city, Melbourne. At a reception for his team in the Melbourne Town Hall, he said: 'If I have something to say now it is only because I have at heart the improvement of cricket, which I love and adore ... We have to set an example, and now I am going to ask you a question: do you think it is quite dignified that the greatest cricket match in the world between the two greatest cricketing powers should be interrupted by a certain amount of noise?' At another reception on the same day, however, the Victorian Attorney-General, Robert Menzies, said: 'Whether Englishmen hit out or sit on the splice, we will have the satisfaction of barracking them. It is our prerogative.' The English team was reported to have joined in the laughter at the remark.

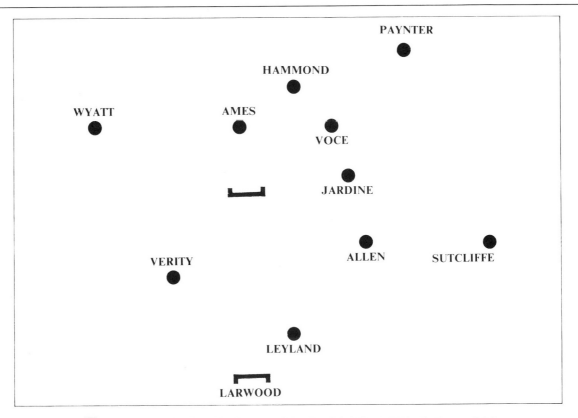

The bodyline field set for Larwood in the third Test. This field was fairly standard, although occasionally Jardine had six men in the inner legside cordon, instead of the five shown here. This diagram was prepared by Pelham Warner for a book he wrote 10 years later. The two deep legside fieldsmen were actually further from the bat than this diagram would suggest. Warner himself noted that they were within 20 yards of the boundary.

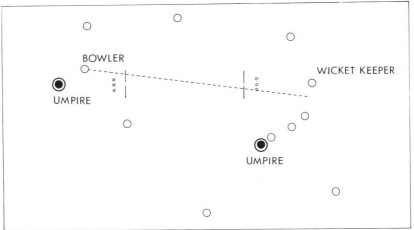

In an attempt to defend the fairness of bodyline bowling, some Englishmen, including Jardine, pointed to the fact that similar methods had often been used in first-class cricket before without attracting criticism. It was true that leg-theory, including fast leg-theory, had been used at various times over the years — although without the attempt at intimidation which Australians insisted was crucial to bodyline's success. The above diagram, which appeared in the *Sydney Referee* in February 1904, shows how the English bowler George Hirst had his field placed in a match then against New South Wales. Apart from the fact that there are only three close fieldsmen in the legside trap, the field is very similar to the one set by Jardine, not only in the arrangement of the inner legside cordon but also in the positioning of the silly mid-on and the two deep fieldsmen on the legside. The diagram also shows that Hirst bowled from wide of the stumps and angled the ball into the batsman — just as Larwood and Voce did nearly 30 years later. It is interesting to recall that the English captain who set the field for Hirst was none other than Pelham Warner.

There were two parts to Jardine's bodyline strategy — a special kind of field setting and a special kind of bowling. Each would have been useless without the other.

A typical bodyline field consisted of a cordon of five close fieldsmen extending from leg slip to silly mid-on. Behind them, another two were stationed near the long-leg boundary.

This meant there were only two fieldsmen on the offside. Les Ames, the English wicketkeeper in the bodyline Tests, can remember a few occasions when there were six fieldsman in the legside cordon, leaving only one fieldsman on the offside.

Bodyline bowling, as defined by Australian batsmen who faced it, consisted of fast, short-pitched deliveries directed straight at the batsman, which meant a high proportion of them bounced at the batsman's hip, chest and head.

The theory was that the Australian batsman would not only be forced to play the ball if it was coming straight at him, but would be forced to play it towards the legside cordon, where sooner or later a catch would result. If he tried to hook the ball over the cordon, he ran the risk of being caught by the two fieldsmen in the deep.

Both Jardine's principal bodyline bowlers, Larwood and Voce, moved the ball off the pitch towards the leg, with the result that the ball was angled into the batsman, making it even harder to deal with. If a batsman tried pulling away, the ball seemed to follow him.

There is some doubt about the above picture.
It was taken at the Sydney Cricket Ground,
Larwood is the bowler and Woodfull is the batsman at the bowler's end.
The batsman is possibly Bradman but more probably Ponsford,
which would identify the Test as the first.
The fieldsmen, from left, appear to be:
Voce, Pataudi (at third man), Allen, Ames (wicketkeeper),
Verity, Jardine and, at far right, Sutcliffe or Hammond.

This effect was accentuated by the fact that Larwood bowled from near the return crease and Voce, a left-arm bowler, often bowled round the wicket.

Australian batsmen objected bitterly to bodyline on the grounds that intimidation was the essence of it. They believed it was wholly dependent on the fear of injury it produced in batsmen. Jack Fingleton said: 'Bodyline demanded an occasional hit or near miss. It was part of the plan and inherent in its nature.'

Jardine and the men who bowled bodyline for him denied emphatically that the bowling was aimed at the Australian batsmen. They claimed it was simply directed at the leg stump and was therefore no different in principle from other leg-theory attacks which had been employed occasionally in the previous 30 years.

One Australian batsman, Vic Richardson, claimed he proved once and for all this was not so. He said that when he took guard on the leg stump during the Adelaide Test he found the ball coming straight at him. When he progressively moved his guard as much as a foot outside the leg stump the ball still came at him.

There were other conflicts of opinion between those who faced bodyline and those who delivered it. For instance, Larwood says that on average he bowled about two bouncers in an (eight-ball) over. However, the Australian batsman Bill Ponsford today says there was an average of four to five bouncers an over while the bodyline field was set.

This was one of Don Bradman's first appearances on the field in that fateful summer of 1932–33. He leads the St George club team onto Rawson Oval for a match against Mosman. Bradman was in great form early in the season. In St George's first match, against Gordon, he made 108, his century coming up in 64 minutes. Then, against Mosman, he made 105 not out, and by the middle of October he had also made 145 in 105 minutes in the first of the New South Wales trials. This last innings included 23 fours and two sixes.

Harold Larwood, in formal pose. Bradman rated him the fastest bowler he ever faced over a full season. 'At times he attained exceptional speed,' Bradman wrote. Larwood bowled faster in 1932–33 than he ever had before, which must be considered unusual. After all, he had turned 28 just as the tour was getting under way, and fast bowlers of that age are invariably losing speed, not gaining it. Larwood's own explanation of his extra pace in 1932–33 is simply that he was fitter than before and was able to get a better foothold.

George Duckworth (above left) had been
England's number-one wicketkeeper on the
1928–29 tour (Ames was his understudy then)
and for the Tests in England in 1930. In
1932–33, however, Ames was chosen for the
Tests instead, and Duckworth had to be content
in playing the minor matches.

Although Gubby Allen (above) refused to bowl
bodyline himself, he nevertheless had a lot of
respect for the ability of the two men who did,
Larwood and Voce. Allen says it required
considerable skill to bowl bodyline
successfully — accuracy as well as pace. He
believes Dennis Lillee, but not Jeff Thomson,
could have been a good bodyline bowler.

On his previous visit to Australia in 1928–29,
Wally Hammond (left) scored 905 runs in the
Tests — a world record which Don Bradman
broke in 1930 by amassing 974 runs. Hammond
seemed to have continued in a similar vein in the
first Test in 1932–33, scoring a solid 112.

Lisle Nagel in action. Commentators criticized him for not bringing his arm right over, thus squandering the advantage of his great height. Having raised hopes that he might be a force against Jardine's men, he was dropped after the first Test and faded into comparative obscurity.

Lisle Nagel, the tall Victorian medium-pace bowler who caused a sensation early in the season by taking 8 English wickets for 32 runs at Melbourne in the match between the MCC and an Australian XI. In one 68-minute period before lunch, he took 6 for 21. The MCC was all out for 60, the lowest score by an English team in Melbourne for nearly 50 years. *The London Evening Standard* quoted Nagel as saying: 'Cricket is a curious game. The wind helped me to swing the ball. That is the only reason for my success.' Then 27 years old, Nagel was 6 feet 6 inches tall, but his action did not allow him to make full use of his height. His eight wickets earned him a place in the first Test, but he never again reproduced the form he showed in Melbourne.

Bob Wyatt, the English vice-captain,
who led the MCC when bodyline was first used
against Bradman in the match against an Australian Eleven in Melbourne.
Jardine had taken a few days off to go fishing.

BATSMEN OUT			FALL OF WKTS.		BAT
WYATT	C 2	3	1 FOR	4	BOW
SUTCLIFFE	B 2	10	2 "	19	VO
LEYLAND	B 2	6	3 "	22	EX
ALLEN	L.B 2	6	4 "	30	9
PAYNTER	B 2	12	5 "	44	ANAL
LARWOOD	C 2	0	6 "	44	1ST I
BROWN	B 4	10	7 "	55	2ND
PATAUDI	C 2	5	8 "	55	EN
DUCKWORTH	L.B 2	4	9 "	59	1ST
			10 "		2ND

The scoreboard at the Melbourne Cricket Ground immediately after the last MCC wicket had fallen for only 60 runs in the Englishmen's match against an Australian XI.
The Englishmen were routed by the Victorian swing bowler Lisle Nagel, who took 8 for 32.

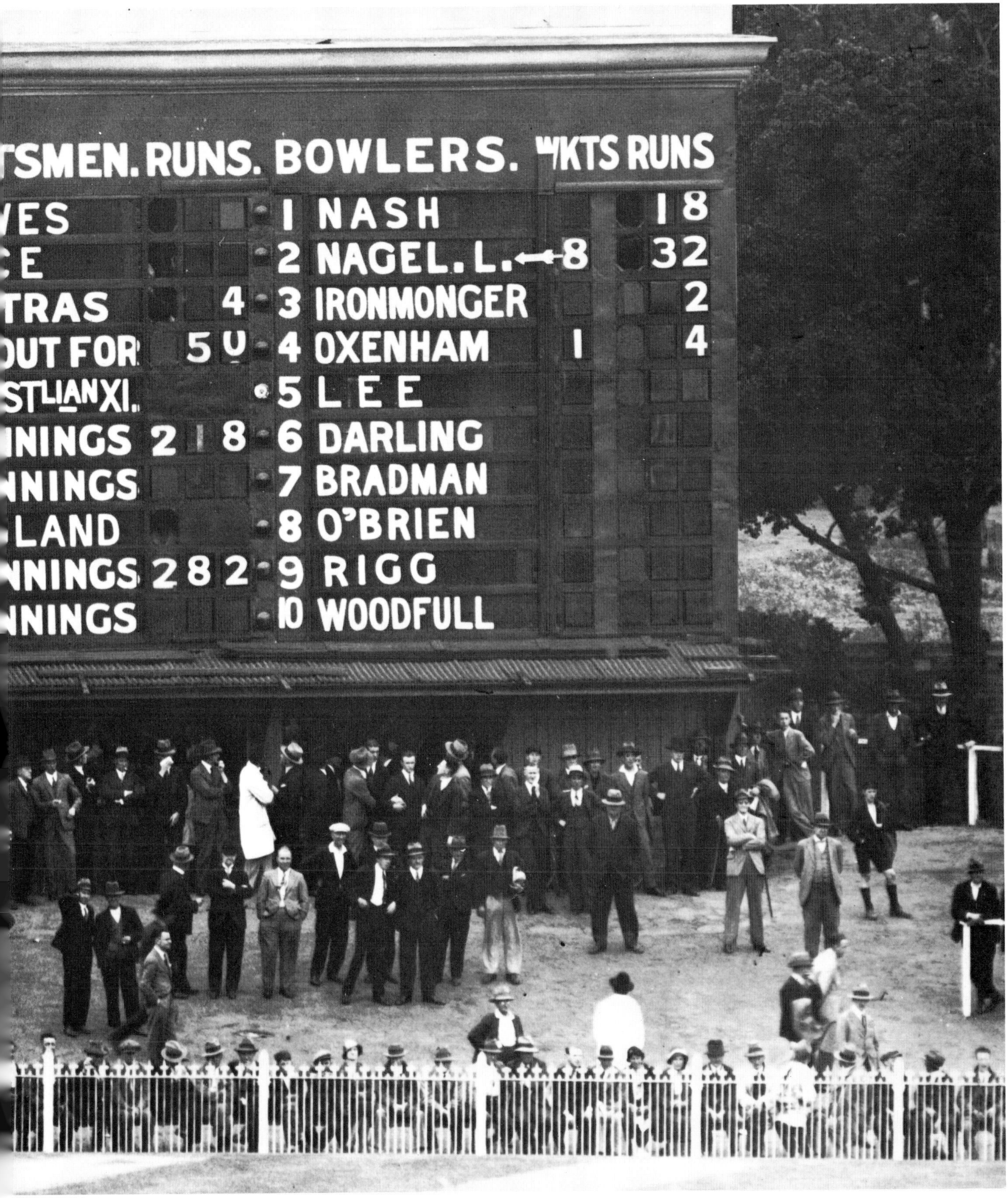
TSMEN. RUNS. BOWLERS. WKTS RUNS
VES 1 NASH 18
E 2 NAGEL. L. 8 32
TRAS 4 3 IRONMONGER 2
OUT FOR 50 4 OXENHAM 1 4
STLIANXI. 5 LEE
NINGS 2 8 6 DARLING
NNINGS 7 BRADMAN
LAND 8 O'BRIEN
NNINGS 282 9 RIGG
NNINGS 10 WOODFULL

Power

. . . in Bradman's batting
and in Plume's performance

*. . . The flash of a willow blade
. . . then, "KLUP!" . . . (Ha!
that satisfying sound of well-
smitten leather!) all the well-
timed power of Bradman behind
it . . . the pickets rattle . . . the
crowd applauds . . . the Umpire
waves . . . "A BOUNDARY!"*

A century maker is he who
has *power* to drive and keep on
driving . . . to speed the flying ball
with flashing cuts and glances . . . and
stand up to express deliveries the hot
summer's day through. Plume too has the
power, the *driving power*, that will enable
you to take the hills in top, the *power*
that means maximum mileage. Plume's
power, proved in every motoring test,
stamps it the champion among motor
spirits.

PLUME

for all-round performance

Starting
Acceleration
Speed
Power
Mileage

VACUUM OIL COMPANY PTY. LTD.

This advertisement appeared in Australian newspapers during the summer of 1932–33.

Young spectators with lunches wrapped in brown paper queue outside the
Sydney Cricket Ground to see New South Wales' first match against the
Englishmen in November 1932. The minimum admission fees fixed by the Board
of Control for the Tests that summer were 2 shillings for the outer and 3 shillings
6 pence for the grandstands. Children were half price. The grounds were entitled,
of course, to charge more than this. For the first Test at Sydney, for instance,
admission to the grandstands cost 4 shillings — a considerable proportion of the
average weekly wage of the day.

Four Victorian cricketers at a Kensington race meeting in Sydney in November
1932. From left they are the fast bowler Harry Alexander, J. Thomas, Len
Darling, who played in two of the bodyline Tests, and Bill Ponsford. (The man in
the middle with the binoculars is a racing official named J. Underhill). The
inclusion of Alexander in the last Test of the series was the nearest Australia
came to retaliating against bodyline. Nicknamed 'Bull', Alexander was strong,
aggressive and quite fast. Encouraged by the Sydney crowd, he frequently pitched
the ball short at Jardine. On one occasion, he struck Jardine a blow in the side
which *The Sydney Morning Herald* described as 'sickening'. 'Immediately there
was a roar from the crowd,' the *Herald* said, 'and then, while some of the
fieldsmen approached Jardine, many of the spectators joined in sustained
applause. Such conduct was unpardonable.'

Jack Fingleton (left) and O. Wendell Bill walk out to open the innings in New South Wales' first match against the MCC. Hit frequently in the body by Voce (Larwood was not playing), Fingleton hung on gamely while NSW wickets fell rapidly, eventually carrying his bat for 119 runs. Fingleton thus became the first Australian to achieve real success against Jardine's new tactics, although, in view of Larwood's absence, he cannot be said to have mastered them. Fingleton later said he experienced no pleasure, but only disillusionment, from his first successful encounter with bodyline.

Voce (above) was yards slower than Larwood, but the Australians found him extremely difficult to handle. This was partly because he generally bowled round the wicket and angled his short-pitched deliveries into the right-handed batsmen.

Fingleton was by no means an exciting batsman to watch,
but he could score freely on occasions.
This is a photograph of him batting in a club match in Sydney.

Don Bradman consoles Jack Fingleton after he is hit by a Voce bouncer
during his innings of 119 for New South Wales.
The English players in the picture are
Pataudi (picking up Fingleton's bat), Ames and Jardine.

Bradman goes down under a Voce bouncer in New South Wales' first match against
the MCC. Larwood did not play in this match,
but Voce made the ball fly at the NSW batsmen,
incurring the wrath of the spectators on the Hill for the first of many times that summer.
Bradman had been ill during the match
and Sydney newspapers credited him with much courage for even making an
appearance at the crease.
He was bowled by Voce for 23 when, in apparent expectation of a bouncer,
he moved to the off to avoid a short-pitched ball,
only to have his middle stump knocked over behind his back.

Two South Australians, Vic Richardson (left) and Tim Wall (right),
arrive at Sydney's Central Station to play in the first Test.
The man between them is unidentified.

Herbert Sutcliffe, England's opening batsman, made a slow 194 in the first Test — an innings which exasperated spectators on the Hill but probably ensured his side's victory. When he was 43 he played defensively at O'Reilly, but the ball slithered off his bat into the base of the stumps without dislodging the bails. That the ball hit the stumps with some force is evident from the distance it bounced back towards the popping crease. The expressions of Grimmett (left) and Oldfield reveal the Australians' disappointment. Bill O'Reilly still thinks that Sutcliffe's remarkable luck may have had important consequences for the whole series. He reasons that if Sutcliffe had been out then Australia might well have gone on to win the Test. Then, if Australia had won the second Test and gone two up in the series, Jardine might have felt compelled to abandon bodyline and revert to orthodox methods.

Jardine, left, and Woodfull tossing. Woodfull won the toss in all Tests except the third.

An aerial photograph taken during the first Test, showing the Sydney Cricket Ground crowded with spectators. At the time, trams ran outside the ground and a big, natural sandhill still dominated the carpark opposite. The Hill, whence much of the barracking against Jardine's men emanated, is the rising slope in front of the scoreboard, at bottom left. At bottom right is the so-called Paddington Hill, also a vantage place for barrackers. It disappeared in the early 1970s when the Bradman Stand was built there.

Part of the crowd at the first Test in Sydney. This picture was taken from the Sheridan Stand and shows the old Brewongle Stand and, beyond it, the Ladies Pavilion. Note the gaps in the paling fence. Hundreds of palings were ripped off by spectators sitting behind the fence who wanted a better view of McCabe's innings of 187 not out.

Stan McCabe at the time of his great innings in the first Test, when he still had a youthful figure. In the years that followed he steadily put on weight, so that by the end of the 1930s he had developed a moon face and a rounded waist.

McCabe hitting to leg during his marvellous innings of 187 not out in the first Test.

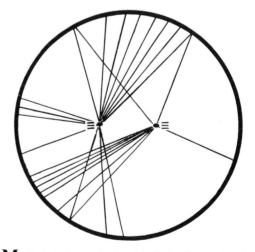

McCabe's boundaries in his innings of 187 not out. Note that a big majority of them were pulls and hooks — strokes which Bradman had decided were too risky to play when the bodyline field was set. The fact that McCabe was successful on this one occasion confirms his own view that he had been very lucky.

McCabe hits Verity for four during his innings of 187. Hammond is at slip.

The English players applaud McCabe (capless) almost as enthusiastically as did the huge Sydney crowd as he leaves the field undefeated on 187, at the end of the Australian innings. Tim Wall is the other batsman. McCabe and Wall added 55 runs in thirty-three minutes for the last wicket, and Wall's contribution to this was only 4. McCabe's 187 was scored in just over four hours and included 25 fours.

Bill O'Reilly as a young schoolteacher. Bill Bowes, like most Englishmen, had tremendous respect for his ability. According to Bowes, after their victory in 1932–33 the English cricketers were confident they would maintain their dominance over Australia. 'Man for man, with the exception of Bradman, we thought we had the advantage,' he wrote, 'and our combined strength made us firm favourites. But we reckoned without the Sydney schoolmaster, Bill O'Reilly. Like Bradman with the bat he proved himself a world-beater with the ball. These were the two men who kept Australia in front during the thirties. They just tipped the scales on the Australian side.'

Lady Game the wife of the New South Wales Governor, Sir Philip Game. The Games were English, of course, and on 1 December, the day before the first Test, they had the English players to lunch at Government House. This is the account Lady Game gave of the occasion in a letter to England: 'We had all the English team to lunch three days ago and it was quite a success I think. We asked the prettiest girls in Sydney to meet (them) and (there) were 37 altogether and I got the whole table done with Australian wild flowers, really lovely ones, and I had 22 little dolls dressed in white flannels as cricketers — 11 with Australian caps and 11 with English. Then we all concocted a menu together which will amuse you I think! And I ordered ices made like a bat and ball on a cricket pitch. This was a secret and everyone was enormously amused when they came in! I had Jardine next to me and liked him so much.' Here, Lady Game underlined the word 'so'. The menu she referred to, incidentally, included items such as Plums Warner and Fruits de Jardine.

'Don't worry ... I will be as right as pie,' Don Bradman is reported to have said when asked about the coming Tests. In fact, he was deeply worried about his and the other Australians' prospects against bodyline, and he may already have concluded that bodyline could not be mastered. Bradman certainly came to this conclusion later. In an ABC radio interview a few years ago, he said: 'The man never lived who could consistently and successfully combat the 1932–33 bodyline attack.'

Johnnie Moyes (left) and Don Bradman, with an unidentified player (possibly a Sydney grade cricketer) between them. Moyes was one of Australia's best-known cricket identities. A former Sheffield Shield player, Moyes wrote many cricket books and for more than 20 years was an ABC cricket broadcaster. He befriended Bradman when the latter first came to Sydney, and it was to Moyes that Bradman turned for advice when he was trying to work out a way of countering bodyline. In his book *Bradman,* Moyes describes how Bradman carefully considered all possibilities, eliminating them one by one. Bradman was confident he could safely dodge Larwood's bouncers, but he realized that the Australian crowds would not be content with this and would demand that he make runs. He ruled out the pull shot against Larwood because of that bowler's tendency to move the ball in, which made the risk of injury great. He ruled out the hook shot, believing he was too short to get on top of the bouncers and keep them down. 'He would walk away from his wicket and try to hit the ball through the offside field,' Moyes wrote. 'If he succeeded it would put the bowler off his balance and would force him to weaken the leg field and strengthen the off field. Then he could revert to normal batsmanship. His plan was, in effect, to meet unorthodoxy with unorthodoxy — he must make runs.'

Bradman bowled first ball by Bowes. Note how wide of the stumps he finished his stroke. A few seconds after this picture was taken, Jardine, the fieldsman at short-leg, danced about in a circle with joy. The next match in which Bowes bowled Bradman was the fourth Test in England in 1934. Then, however, Bradman had scored 304.

A close-up of Bradman's famous duck.

Bradman's famous pull shot — as demonstrated for a 1934 coaching manual. This is the kind of stroke which Bradman was attempting when he was bowled by Bowes.

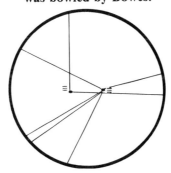

Bradman's boundaries in his innings of 103 not out. One of his pull shots for four that day has been recorded on an old newsreel film. It was a stroke of tremendous power, which Bradman played leaning back on a bent right knee, and the ball sped to the boundary in a series of low bounds.

The Anglo-Indian batsman, the Nawab of Pataudi, who seems to have been a reluctant participant in the bodyline strategy. There was a story told on the Australian side that during the second Test he refused to move into the bodyline trap when Jardine directed him there, whereupon Jardine made the sarcastic remark: 'His Excellency is a conscientious objector.'

Alan Kippax, the stylish New South Wales batsman who was reckoned to be one of the leading players of his era, faced bodyline in the first Test and immediately confided to his teammates that he felt he had faced enough of it. Kippax had been badly injured in the previous season when he was hit on the head in a match against Queensland, and his confidence against fast bowling, particularly short-pitched bowling, was shaken. Moreover, he was now 35 years old, and his reflexes, presumably, were not as sharp as they had been. All this is a pity, for in his first book, *Don Bradman's Book,* Bradman said Kippax was the best hooker he had seen. Kippax made 8 and 19 in the first Test, falling both times to Larwood, and he was not included in another Test side that series.

BRADMAN'S CENTURY

Cheered by Englishmen.

BRILLIANT INNINGS.

Crowd's Great Demonstration.

DOGGED FIGHT FOR THE TEST.

Many Australian Batsmen Fail.

WORLD'S RECORD ATTENDANCE OF 68,188.

(FROM OUR SPECIAL REPRESENTATIVE.)

MELBOURNE, Monday.

England requires to reach a total of 251 in the second innings to win the second test match with Australia at the Melbourne Cricket Ground. Batting for three-quarters of an hour this afternoon, Sutcliffe and Leyland made 43 of the runs, and all wickets are intact.

Australia again surprisingly failed with the bat, scoring only 191 in the second innings. The team was saved from utter collapse by Don Bradman, who played a magnificent fighting innings. He passed his century with the last man in amid the greatest enthusiasm, and was 103 not out when the innings ended.

The Englishmen performed splendidly on a wicket which did not assist the fast bowlers. Hammond made an excellent effort, taking three wickets for 21 runs, and Larwood, Allen, and Voce all contributed to the good work.

Bradman showed that the wicket was easy enough, but it should prove of more assistance to Australia's spin bowlers than it was to the men of pace.

A world's record crowd of 68,188 was thrilled by a day's play full of incident.

The headline Australians had been longing to read (from *The Sydney Morning Herald*)

Woodfull bowled by Allen for 10 in the second Test.

This picture of O'Reilly was published after the second Test, in which he took five wickets in each innings and so played a big part in Australia's victory. The journalist R. W. E. Wilmot gave the following account of an exchange between O'Reilly and an umpire during that Test: '"How is your eyesight today?" said W. J. O'Reilly to one of the umpires in Melbourne. "All right," was the reply. "How is your hearing?" was the second question. The answer was equally prompt: "It's all right, too." "You'll need them both," replied O'Reilly, "for I am after them today, and I want plenty of wickets".'

Bill Bowes was probably England's biggest disappointment of the tour, for he was never able to reproduce his form of the previous summer in England. Bowes played in only one Test and took only one wicket, but what a wicket it was — Don Bradman bowled first ball for a duck.

After his brilliant 187 not out in the first Test, McCabe found himself no better able than the other Australian batsmen to cope with bodyline. His Tests scores after that first great innings were: 32, 32, 0, 8, 7, 20, 22, 73, 4. If he had not begun the series in a blaze of glory, there is every chance he would have been dropped from the team, as Fingleton and Ponsford were.

After making 32 and 2 in the first Test, Bill Ponsford was made 12th man for the second. The selectors — E. A. Dwyer of New South Wales, Dr C. E. Dolling of South Australia and W. Johnson of Victoria — had already made it clear they were not taking reputations into account by dropping Alan Kippax. Kippax had made 8 and 19 in the first Test.

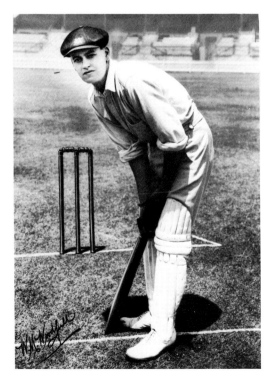

A stylized portrait of Bill Woodfull. This is how the journalist R. W. E. Wilmot viewed Woodfull's attempts to deal with the bodyline attack: 'Woodfull, never quick on his feet, faced it, but ducked his head and often his body, and was frequently struck. Twice — once in Melbourne and once in Adelaide — he was hit over the heart, but in each case it was by a ball well-pitched up, which fizzed and kicked, and he could not avoid it. His stubbornness and his courage were remarkable.'

Sutcliffe and Wyatt. This pair opened England's batting in the first two Tests, but Wyatt later dropped himself down the order to let Jardine open instead. Wyatt had an excellent series, scoring 327 runs in the Tests at an average of 46·7.

After his unhappy encounters with bodyline early in the season, Alan Kippax (left) became one of its strongest critics. Later in 1933, he helped write a book condemning it, which bore his name as author. In the book, called *Anti Body-Line,* Kippax wrote: 'Some idea of what body-line methods would produce in the lower grades of cricket has already been obtained in Australia. After the first match, England v New South Wales, the tactics were adopted in many junior games the following Saturday. There are over 30,000 juniors playing every Saturday in Sydney alone, practically all on concrete wickets. The immediate result of body-line bowling in these matches may be summarised. On Moore Park, Sydney, a batsman walked down the pitch and threatened to hit the bowler over the head with the bat. On the Domain, a match lasted 15 minutes, ending in a free-fight between the opposing teams. In Adelaide junior cricket, a match was abandoned for a similar brawl after ten minutes' play. Similar reports were received from country centres. The ambulance officer on duty at Centennial Park, Sydney, reported that his casualty list on that day was four times its usual length, the vast majority of the additions being head injuries. Such is bodyline bowling in practice.'

The climactic third Test at Adelaide begins.
Bill Woodfull leads the Australian team onto the field on the morning of the first day.
Vic Richardson is immediately behind him.

Bill Woodfull clutches his chest and staggers from the wicket after being hit by Larwood.
That Woodfull took the full force of the ball is evident from the fact
that it has bounced back towards the bowler.

Another view of Woodfull being hit.
Notice how far back the first-slip, Hammond, is standing.
(A Fishwick Photo)

Woodfull's eventful innings in the Adelaide Test, in which he was hit in the chest
by Larwood, came to an end when he was bowled by Allen. He had made 22.
Two hours later Woodfull delivered his highly publicized rebuke to Pelham
Warner in the Australian dressing room.

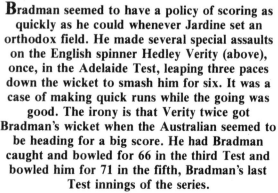

Bradman seemed to have a policy of scoring as quickly as he could whenever Jardine set an orthodox field. He made several special assaults on the English spinner Hedley Verity (above), once, in the Adelaide Test, leaping three paces down the wicket to smash him for six. It was a case of making quick runs while the going was good. The irony is that Verity twice got Bradman's wicket when the Australian seemed to be heading for a big score. He had Bradman caught and bowled for 66 in the third Test and bowled him for 71 in the fifth, Bradman's last Test innings of the series.

The two captains in conference. Relations between them were said to be correct but never cordial. An interesting feature of the bodyline story was Woodfull's refusal to let his bowlers use similar tactics. Of course, there can be no certainty that Australia's leading pace bowlers — Alexander, Wall and McCormick — were either fast or accurate enough to bowl bodyline successfully, but Woodfull had already ruled out the idea of retaliation on principle. Bill O'Reilly remembers him saying that no Australian would bowl bodyline while he was skipper. O'Reilly says there was no agitation among the Australian players for retaliation at the time, although he recalls Vic Richardson saying after the series was over that he would have used bodyline against the Englishmen if he had been captain. This photograph is from the collection of Pat Mullins.

O'Reilly bowling in the third Test. According to the original caption for this picture, the batsman is Hammond, but O'Reilly says he cannot remember Hammond ever playing a swish of this kind. He thinks the batsman is possibly Ames. The other Australians in the picture are, from left, McCabe in slips, Richardson (who kept wickets after Oldfield was injured), O'Brien (twelfth man) (A Fishwick Photo)

A close-up of the picture above.

This is another picture taking during the third Test in which the identity of the batsman is in doubt. The original caption names him as Hammond, yet he looks remarkably like Ames. There is no doubt about the wicketkeeper — Bert Oldfield. (A Fishwick Photo)

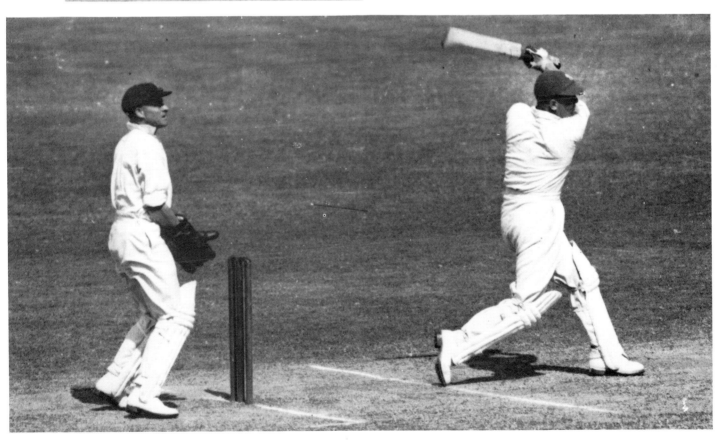

A prolific scorer throughout most of his career, Bill Ponsford was unable to cope with the bodyline attack and was dropped from the Test side twice during the series. He did have a few hours of glory, however. In the third Test at Adelaide, when Larwood was at his most venemous and dangerous, Ponsford ground out 85 runs, thereby saving the Australian innings from complete disintegration. Ponsford adopted the tactic of turning his back into the rising balls, and by the end of the innings was badly bruised. 'When I got under the shower, Vic Richardson drew everyone's attention to it,' he says. The bruises were darkest just under his left shoulder blade.

Tim Wall was probably the best of the fast bowlers Australia was able to put in the field against Jardine's men, but he could not match Larwood for pace, nor Voce for venom. It is doubtful, therefore, that he could have bowled bodyline successfully in retaliation, even if Woodfull had wanted him to. Bradman, at the end of his career, wrote that Wall was the finest fast bowler he ever faced while the ball was new. 'He had a wonderful ability to make it swing late,' Bradman said. 'I recall Archie Jackson in Adelaide one year trying to leg-glance a ball from Tim, and then in bewilderment looking round to see his off-bail on the ground.' Wall's best performance in the bodyline Tests was 5 for 72 in the controversial Adelaide match.

Bradman ducks a bouncer from Larwood
during the third Test. For running such a high
risk of being bruised by bodyline, the
Australians were paid at the rate of £30 a Test
plus a 25-shilling allowance. This was less than
they received in 1928–29, when as well as the
match fee of £30 they were paid a £10 bonus.

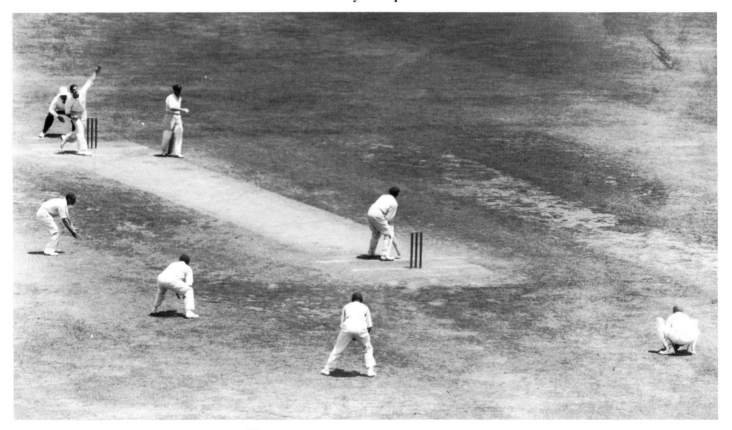

Voce bowls to Ponsford in the third Test.
The other batsmen is probably Oldfield.
Ponsford was later bowled behind his legs by Voce for 85.
The fieldsmen, from left, are Allen, Hammond and Jardine.
Ames is the wicketkeeper.

Bill Woodfull and Vic Richardson. Woodfull had no regrets about his sharp
rebuke to Warner in the Australian dressing room. On the Monday of the
Adelaide Test, after the incident had been reported in the newspapers, Warner
made this statement to the press: 'Woodfull has expressed regret to Mr Palairet
(the English team's co-manager) and myself, and we are now all good friends.'
But later in the day Woodfull issued the following statement through the Board's
secretary, Jeanes: 'I did not apologize to Mr Warner for any statement I made. I
merely told him the matter was not a personal one between himself and myself. I
strongly repudiate any suggestion that I tendered any apology to Mr Warner for
any statement I made.' This picture of Richardson, incidentally, shows that his
grandson, Ian Chappell, inherited not only his talent for cricket but many of his
looks. (A Fishwick Photo)

Two men at the centre of the turmoil —
the Board's chairman, Dr Robertson, and Jack Fingleton.

After faring so well against bodyline in the earlier matches, Jack Fingleton made two ducks in the Adelaide Test and was dropped from the Australian side. Fingleton might well have considered he was harshly treated by the selectors, for his scores had been creditable enough in the first two Tests — 26, 40, 83 and 1.

Three prominent Board of Control officials in 1933: from left — Bill Jeanes, secretary; Aubrey Oxlade, chairman; and Frank Cush, a NSW delegate. Cush, incidentally, played an important part in furthering Don Bradman's early career. He was secretary of the St George Club, which Bradman joined when he started playing in Sydney. Bradman, when he first moved to the city, also lived for some time at his home.

The injury to Oldfield happened on the Monday of the Adelaide Test, when the situation was already inflamed. Oldfield had made 41 when he swung at a short ball from Larwood, missed it and was struck on the right temple. He dropped his bat, staggered a few paces from the pitch and sank to his knees. The English players, including Larwood, gathered about him, and Gubby Allen ran off the field to get a jug of water and a towel. When he returned he was followed by the Australian captain, Woodfull. Newsreel films of the incident show Woodfull striding out on the field with his shoulders back, as if he were seething with anger. Larwood had been bowling to Oldfield with a bodyline field, and Woodfull, like many other Australians, no doubt considered this unfair tactics to use against a number-seven batsman. Oldfield was soon back on his feet, but immediately left the field and took no further part in the match. An X-ray showed later than his skull had been fractured. On Tuesday, Mrs Oldfield in Sydney received a telegram from Jardine, expressing his regrets on behalf of the English team.

Voce bowls to Woodfull with a reduced legside field. Ponsford is the other batsman.

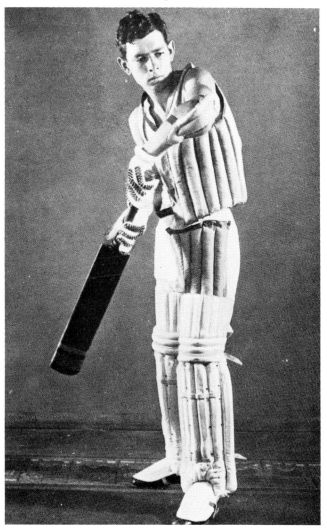

Several Australian batsmen took to wearing thigh,
body and even elbow padding.
This is said to be the padding used by Jack Fingleton.

Bill Ponsford. He decided upon the most desperate of all methods of playing bodyline — turning his back into the bouncers — but it was successful for him only once, when he made 85 in the third Test at Adelaide. More than once he had his leg stump knocked over behind his back after moving out of the line of the ball to the off.

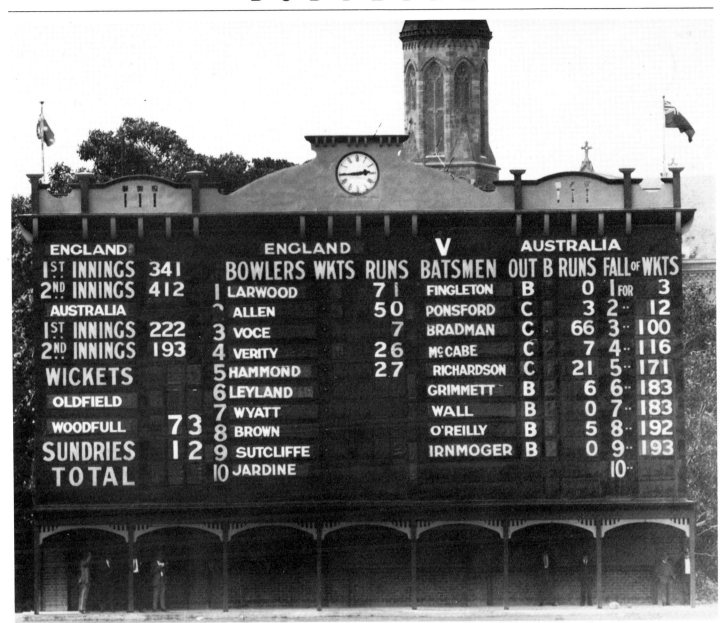

The scoreboard at Adelaide showing a win for England after the third Test.
(A Fishwick Photo)

Bert Oldfield, with head still bandaged, back at home in Sydney with his wife, Ruth, and their two daughters, following his injury at Adelaide. It does not seem to have ever been recorded that Jardine made a most touching gesture of regret to Oldfield after he was injured. He had a friend of his deliver two Shirley Temple dolls to Oldfield's home as gifts for his daughters.

Bert Oldfield absolved Larwood of blame for his injury in Adelaide. A few days after the Test he told a reporter: 'I do not wish anyone to accept the consequences of my mistake. In this particular instance, Larwood was not to blame, as the ball that hit me was pitched in line with the wicket, short; and somehow I lost sight of it after the ball hit the pitch. The next thing I knew it had hit me. I had been dodging his fliers, but I lost this ball, which was rather unfortunate.'

Bill Woodfull, as he was seen by the English bowlers. The only time he lost control of himself throughout the bodyline series was when Pelham Warner came to the Australian dressing room to express regrets for the blow to the chest Woodfull had earlier received from Larwood. This is Warner's account of the incident: 'Our reception was freezing. Woodfull has just had a shower-bath, and we found him with a towel wrapped around him, and the following conversation passed. We said how sorry we were, and Woodfull replied, "I don't want to see you, Mr Warner. There are two teams out there. One is trying to play cricket and the other is not." I replied, "Apart from all that, we most sincerely hope you are not too badly hurt," and he answered, "The bruise is coming out," and there certainly was a very livid mark over his heart. We then left the room ... We had always been good friends, and frankly I did not expect the reception we received.' Warner was accused of tactlessness in going to see Woodfull too soon after he had been hit, but Warner later claimed that he had, in fact, deliberately waited two hours to allow feelings to calm down. Warner also claimed, with justification, that he would have laid himself open to criticism if he had not gone to express his regrets.

Pelham Warner in Australia in 1932–33. In some ways he was bodyline's
unhappiest victim of all, however much he might deserve to be criticized for not
taking a stronger stand against it. The controversy affected him deeply, because
he was a great believer in tradition. This is what he once said to an Australian
reporter on the subject of tradition and the old school tie: 'They've got it all
wrong in Australia, you know. It means nothing more than loyalty to the scene of
your happy schooldays, no more than being proud of getting your colours in the
Australian eleven. You owe a lot to your school and the friends you made there.
You thank God that you went to such a place. This modern scoffing at tradition
is a product of super-democracy. Tradition is a hell of a good thing. It's what
takes a regiment through hell. Good God, you fellows out in Australia have a
great tradition. What fighters you are! What is it, do you think, that makes your
soldiers fight to the last man and your cricketers to the last ball? It's tradition, of
course. I'm a great believer in it.'

Les Ames was one of several English players who has misgivings about the bodyline tactics but refrained from questioning them out of loyalty to Jardine. Bill Ponsford has a clear memory today of Ames going out of his way to sympathize with him when he took a battering from the English fast bowlers in the third Test.

Gubby Allen (pictured here in November 1932) was a confidant of Pelham Warner throughout the tour. On the evening of the Monday of the Adelaide Test — the day Oldfield was hit on the head — Warner had a meeting with members of the Board of Control and was then reported to have had a 'long talk' with Allen. Allen was Australian-born, and Warner later wrote of the hospitality he received that summer from several of Allen's relatives in Australia.

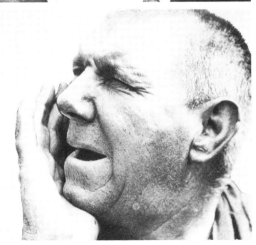

Stephen Gascoigne of Sydney, better known as Yabba, was the only Australian barracker who became a celebrity in his own right. The reason for this, apparently, was that he had a tremendously powerful voice, which could be heard over the whole ground. Harold Larwood, who knew his voice well, says it could be heard clearly on the side of the ground farthest from the Hill, which was Yabba's usual haunt. Whether, as some claim, it was Yabba who told Jardine to 'leave our bloody flies alone' when the English captain was brushing flies from his face or whether, as others claim, it was actually a barracker at Adelaide Oval, has never been established.

The Prime Minister, Joseph Lyons, conducted
his bodyline diplomacy by telephone, speaking to
the British Government's representative in
Australia, Ernest Crutchley, the Board of
Control's chairman, Dr Robertson, and,
presumably, advisers within his own
Government. Lyons was of Irish extraction but
was a monarchist and an Anglophile. His
daughter, Mrs Enid Austin, can vouch for his
interest in cricket. She remembers him inviting
English cricketers to his home in 1936–37 and
staying up late at night to listen to radio
broadcasts of the Tests in England. He also
played cricket occasionally, even in his later
years. His home town in Tasmania, Stanley,
used to hold a 'Back to Stanley Week' in his
honour each year, and Lyons sometimes played
in the cricket match that always formed part of
the celebrations.

Sir Alexander Hore-Ruthven, the Governor of
South Australia, who exerted diplomatic
pressure in London to stop the bodyline dispute
worsening. He is shown here playing in a cricket
match, probably in Canberra, in 1939.

Lloyd Dumas, the editor of the *Adelaide
Advertiser,* who was one of the people consulted
by the Acting Governor of South Australia
about ways of taking the heat out of the
bodyline row. It was recognized at the time that
Australian feeling was being inflamed not only
by what was happening on the field but by
comments about it in the British press, many of
which were reproduced in Australian
newspapers. The theme of these comments was
that Australians were 'squealers'. Accordingly,
Dumas was asked to contact Geoffrey Dawson,
the editor of *The Times,* which he later described
as being 'one of the worst offenders'. In a cable
he sent to Dawson, Dumas said: 'Any friendly
comment would greatly help Australian press in
efforts to prevent demonstration. Am cabling
you personally because confident you equally
desirous prevent development bitterness between
two peoples.' Dawson wrote back that he
thought Dumas was reading too much into the
reports of *The Times,* but he agreed that feeling
had to be taken into account and would see that
the relevant people on his staff were made aware
of this. Dumas also wrote to the editors of six
other leading British dailies and to the editors of
all the metropolitan newspapers in Australia,
urging them to use their influence to have peace
restored in the cricket world. His efforts
probably had a lot to do with the subsequent
settlement of the bodyline row. 'When I visited
London in 1935,' Dumas wrote, 'I was
entertained at lunch at The Times and, in a
jocular way, was accused of being a "squealer".
The memory still lingered, but there was no
more sting in it.'

Immediately after the Adelaide Test, several famous cricketers, past and present, played at Rushcutters Bay in Sydney in a match between the Navy and the press. The match provided the interesting spectacle of Jack Hobbs and Don Bradman who were in the press team, batting together. This picture shows Hobbs (left) with Bradman and one Admiral Dalglish.

look four holes in suc
and 15th—to become
kered with his secon
green. Pearce was c
hole and become 1
and Winser, holing
At the 13th Winser
He got out with his
holed another long p
holes seemed somew
takes at the next tv
back at the 16th, bu
where he sliced his c
effort under the tree
In the afternoon
good chance of furth
where he short-putted
putts from 10ft at th
for 2 at the ninth.
6 down at the 10th.
mistake in judging t
12th. I had seen a
just in front of Pear
with a niblick. Pear
into the ti-tree beyor
hole. This left Wir
won the next, but t
appeared, and Winse

THE INTI

ON Thursday the
the morning V
played against
captain of our team
like to play me, I pu
with him. I played f
and just managed to
spoon shot from the
to get a useful 2.
rather used up after
pionship, and little in
to the result, as I h
for three days.
In the afternoor
down badly to Vict
Howard played No. i
plished a fine perfort
2. Howard was I t

Keith Officer, a prominent Australian diplomat. Officer was one Australian Government official who did what he could to put a lid on the controversy; possibly at the direction of the Prime Minister, Joseph Lyons. Gubby Allen can remember him, as a Government representative, discussing the affair with senior members of the English party.

Legh Winser, when he was Australian amateur golf champion. Born in England in November 1887, Winser played cricket for Staffordshire from 1906 to 1909 and, after emigrating to Australia, for South Australia before and after World War I. He once kept wickets in a social match while W.G. Grace was batting, and so must be one of the very few men alive today who played with or against that famous cricketer. Winser was private secretary to the Governor of South Australia when the crisis developed after the Adelaide Test, and he played an active part in the diplomatic manoeuvring which followed. For years he kept copies of the Governor's correspondence on the matter, but in the late 1960s decided to deposit them at Lord's. This has proved an unfortunate decision for Australian historians, for, although 50 years have passed since the letters were written, the MCC will not allow anyone to inspect them. Now only a few years short of his 100th birthday, Legh Winser still swings a golf club occasionally on the front lawn of his home at Barwon Heads, Victoria.

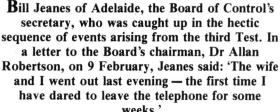

Bill Jeanes of Adelaide, the Board of Control's secretary, who was caught up in the hectic sequence of events arising from the third Test. In a letter to the Board's chairman, Dr Allan Robertson, on 9 February, Jeanes said: 'The wife and I went out last evening — the first time I have dared to leave the telephone for some weeks.'

Syd Smith, of Sydney, the veteran cricket official who had been manager of the Australian teams which toured England in 1921 and 1926. Smith had known cricket controversies before — he was present when two Australian selectors, Clem Hill and Peter McAlister, had their much-publicized fist fight over a selection disagreement in 1912. He strongly criticized the Board of Control's action in sending the initial cable, saying it would make Australians seem like squealers — a fear that was later proved to be justified. When the MCC sent back its sharp reply, Smith said: 'It is the obvious reply to the Board of Control's untimely and crudely-worded cable. Leg-theory bowling is a matter which should have been left in abeyance until the conclusion of the Tests, and then submitted to the MCC for consideration by the Imperial Cricket Conference.' It may be noted here that, apparently in the interests of reconciliation, Smith even refrained from referring to Jardine's methods as bodyline.

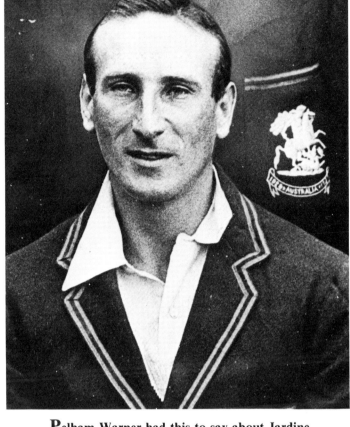

Ernest Crutchley, the British Government's representative in Australia. Although it was the two English managers, Warner and Palairet, who made the initial appeal to Crutchley for help, at least one newspaper of the day reported that the decision to do so was made by the two managers and Jardine. The request to Crutchley was that he should use his influence to get the Board of Control to withdraw the word 'unsportsmanlike', which it had used to describe the English tactics. This was considered essential, if for no other reason than that Jardine had let it be known that he would not lead England in the next Test if the word were not withdrawn. Crutchley decided on drastic action: he went straight to the Australian Prime Minister, Joseph Lyons.

Pelham Warner had this to say about Jardine (above) many years after the bodyline Tests: 'It appears that on his previous visit to Australia with Chapman's MCC team, Jardine had neither understood nor been understood by the Australians. Unfortunately he was not sympatica to them, nor they to him ... Jardine, through a storm of controversy which is quite unparalleled in the history of cricket, refused to bow his head and his courage and determination are not to be gainsaid.'

English fieldsmen crowd H. Chilvers of New South Wales
during the second of the MCC's matches against New South Wales.
The identity of the bowler is not known,
although we may deduce from the position of the wicketkeeper,
Duckworth, that he was a slow or medium-pace bowler.
The fieldsmen, from left, are: Mitchell, Ames, Wyatt and Verity.

Len Darling

Bradman played one of his best innings against Jardine's men in the return
match between New South Wales and the MCC. He made 71 on a wet wicket. He
is seen here driving Hammond, watched by the wicketkeeper, Duckworth.

Sir William McKell, later Premier of New South
Wales and Governor-General of Australia, was
one of many Australians who thought Woodfull
ought to use bodyline against the Englishmen.
Sir William recalls today a conversation he had
with Woodfull on the subject while they were
sitting next to each other at lunch during one of
the Sydney Tests. Sir William raised the matter
by saying that, in his experience as a Rugby
footballer, the only way to counter rough tactics
was to use rough tactics oneself. Whereupon
Woodfull turned to him and said, 'Do you
suggest we should retaliate?' When Sir William
said that was exactly what he was suggesting,
Woodfull dismissed the idea rather testily and
would not discuss it further. Sir William says he
obviously resented the suggestion even being put
to him.

Clarrie Grimmett was another big-name Australian player
for whom 1932–33 proved to be a miserable season.
He played in only three Tests and took only five wickets at an average of 65·2.

Maurice Tate on the Sydney Cricket Ground's number-two oval. This great medium-pace bowler of the 1920s was treated as a spent force by the English selectors on the 1932–33 tour. He played in only five first-class matches on the tour and took only 12 wickets, for his style of bowling had no place in Jardine's strategy.

Although he was never quite considered to be a genuine all-rounder, Stan McCabe was a useful bowler for Australia throughout his career. He was not so successful in the 1932–33 Tests, however. He took only three wickets at an average of 71·7.

Jardine had tremendous respect for Bradman's ability — the fact that he brought bodyline into being is proof of that. He once wrote: 'I feel certain that no one has ever been able to hook better, or to keep the ball down in Bradman's inimitable manner when hooking. His outstanding ability in this respect made his comparative failure against Larwood in Australia seem all the more remarkable.' This is a strange comment, for it was clear to all at the time that Bradman deliberately refrained from playing the hook, having decided it was too risky in view of the bodyline field placements.

Eddie Gilbert, the Queensland Aboriginal bowler whom Bradman rated
the fastest he ever faced over a short period.
In one match against New South Wales, Gilbert actually knocked the bat
from Bradman's hands before getting him out for a duck.
Bradman wrote: 'The ball came through at bewildering speed which seemed to be
accentuated because Gilbert only shuffled about four quick steps before delivering the ball.
One delivery knocked the bat out of my hand,
and I unhesitatingly class this short burst as faster than anything seen from Larwood
or anyone else.'
Gilbert's action was highly suspect, however,
and there was never any real prospect he would be chosen for a Test.
But after the row over bodyline came to a head at Adelaide,
Gilbert was seen by some people as a means of retaliation.
The MCC's first match after Adelaide was against Queensland in Brisbane,
and one Queensland Cricket Association official was quoted as saying
that Gilbert would be instructed to bowl bodyline against the Englishmen
if authorities in England had not responded favourably to the Board of Control's cable.
Asked about the idea, Gilbert said: 'I have absolutely no objection to bowling leg-theory,
and, further, I will get more wickets by doing so.'
In the event, Gilbert did not bowl bodyline.

Many Australians were hoping that the Aboriginal fast bowler Eddie Gilbert
would give Jardine's men some of their own medicine when they came to Brisbane
to play Queensland after the third Test.
Although Gilbert did hit Jardine a severe blow in the side,
the Englishmen handled him comfortably enough.
However, Gilbert did claim a victim in his own team —
the Queensland wicketkeeper who was hit in the stomach
by one of Gilbert's faster deliveries and doubled up in pain.

Jardine plays forward to Ironmonger in the fourth Test at Brisbane.
The close fieldsman on the off is Vic Richardson.
The wicketkeeper here is H. S. B. Love of New South Wales
who replaced the injured Oldfield.

Jardine with two of Australia's leading cricket officials — Syd Smith, left, and Aubrey Oxlade (with pipe). This picture is dated January 1933, and was probably taken when the Englishmen came to Sydney at the end of the month while the furore over the Board of Control's cable was at its height. Both Smith and Oxlade opposed the sending of the cable.

Larwood was the cause of Ponsford's undoing in the fourth Test at Brisbane. He bowled him behind his legs for 19 in the first innings and caught him brilliantly for a duck in the second. Ponsford was dropped for the fifth Test.

Bradman goes down the pitch to drive Verity
during his innings of 76 in the first innings of the fourth Test.

As the above diagram shows, Bradman scored
most of his boundaries on the offside during his
innings of 76 in the fourth Test. It was another
adventurous innings, and for a time Bradman
looked to have much the best of the contest with
Larwood.

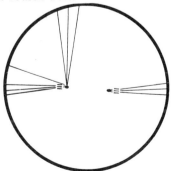

Herbert Sutcliffe scored plenty of boundaries in
his innings of 86 in the fourth Test, but, as this
diagram shows, virtually all of them were scored
behind the wicket.

Richardson driving Verity in the first innings of the fourth Test.
Richardson made a smart 83 in this innings,
his highest score in the series.

Jardine takes one hand off the bat as he sweeps O'Reilly for four in the fourth Test.
The wicketkeeper is H. S. B. Love (replacing the injured Oldfield)
and the fieldsman is Richardson. (A Fishwick Photo).

Len Darling, the Victorian left-hander, cuts Hammond for runs in the fourth Test.
Darling was brought into the team for the fourth Test,
effectively replacing Fingleton, who was dropped
after making two ducks in the third Test. (A Fishwick Photo)

As a tail-end batsman, Bill O'Reilly could be a dangerous hitter on occasions,
but he used strictly safety-first methods when facing Larwood in 1932–33 —
he stepped back a pace or two towards square leg and did his best from there.
This was at the express direction of his captain, Woodfull,
who told O'Reilly at the outset that his first concern had to be avoiding injury.
O'Reilly says he was never so happy to obey any captain's command.
He is seen here standing well to the onside while his off stump is knocked back by Larwood
in the fourth Test at Brisbane.
The fieldsman on the legside is Gubby Allen.

The little English left-hander Eddie Paynter.
Paynter was not included in the team until the third Test,
but he actually headed the Test batting averages for both sides with 61·3,
thanks largely to the fact that he was not out in two of his five Test innings.
In the fourth Test at Brisbane,
Paynter played an innings which Pelham Warner later described as heroic.
Stricken with tonsilitis at the end of the first day's play,
Paynter became so ill and ran such a high temperature that he was
admitted to a nursing home.
Warner later wrote: 'When I told Jardine on the Sunday morning
that it looked very doubtful whether he would be able to bat,
he said, 'What about those fellows who marched to Kandahar with fever on them?'
— a remark which delighted me and was typical of our captain's grit and determination."
Though still weak, Paynter took his place at the crease late on Monday
and was 24 not out at stumps.
He returned to the nursing home that night,
but resumed his innings on Tuesday and went on to make 83.
His innings turned the tide of the match.
"I do not think there has ever been a greater example of grit and guts on the field than this,"
Warner wrote.

Vic Richardson holds a skied catch
— ending Paynter's brave innings of 83 in the fourth Test.

Richardson caught by Jardine off the bowling of Verity for 32 in the fourth Test.

Richardson facing Hammond in the second innings of the fourth Test.

Archie Jackson cover-driving.

Archie Jackson. This highly promising batsman died in Brisbane on the last day of the Test there, aged 23. Jackson rose to prominence in big cricket about the same time as Bradman and for a short time was considered by some to be a rival to Bradman. He was a stylish, graceful batsman out of the Trumper mould, and after he made 164 against England in his first Test in 1928–29 his future seemed assured. His form faltered in England in 1930, however, and towards the end of the following year he was found to be suffering from tuberculosis.

He spent the winter of 1932 resting in the Blue Mountains and his health improved, but in September that year he moved to Brisbane. There, against his doctor's advice, he began playing regular club cricket, and at the end of January, 1933, he collapsed and was taken to hospital. He died there on February 16. During the fourth Test he sent the following telegram to Larwood from his hospital: "Congratulations magnificent bowling. Good luck all matches. Archie Jackson."

A big crowd was outside the Jacksons' family home in Wrights Road, Drummoyne, when the funeral left for the Field of Mars Cemetery. Some weeks later teams of past and present Australian cricketers, including Monty Noble, Herbie Collins and Charlie Macartney, staged a match at the Sydney Cricket Ground to raise money for a Jackson memorial fund. Bradman caused some amusement while bowling in the match by placing a bodyline field and bouncing the ball short in imitation of Larwood. A newspaper reported that one ball bounced four times before it reached the batsman.

Jackson's body was returned to his home city, Sydney, on the same train which brought the Australian players back after the fourth Test. Six of the Australian team acted as pallbears at his funeral. They are shown here led by Richardson (left) and Woodfull. Ponsford and Bradman are behind Richardson, and McCabe and Oldfield are behind Woodfull.

Don Bradman driving in the fifth Test.
(A Fishwick Photo)

Larwood bowling — from a newsreel film taken during the first innings of the fifth Test. These pictures were published in the *Sydney Mail* after the conclusion of the series to support the contention of the *Sydney Mail's* cricket correspondent, Eric Barbour, that Larwood was dragging over the line and therefore bowling no-balls. It may be noted here as a matter of record that a suggestion has occasionally been whispered by some people in Australia that Larwood's action was suspect. Even one former team-mate of Larwood's in England admitted he had heard the suggestion, but discounted it as nonsense. Bill O'Reilly says he is sure the legality of Larwood's action was never once called into question during the series itself, when, according to O'Reilly, many Australians would have been only too eager to have the matter raised. O'Reilly, too, discounts the suggestion as nonsense.

Bradman is bowled by Larwood for 48 in the first innings of the fifth Test.
It was a brief but exciting innings in which Bradman repeatedly
stepped back to hit Larwood to the offside.
He also played some spectacular shots off Allen.
When he was 44, Bradman cut Larwood brilliantly to the boundary,
but against the next ball he moved towards the off to try to glance
and was bowled behind his legs.
Both Bradman and Ponsford were bowled in similar fashion several times that season.

Bodyline claims other victims in the fifth Test at Sydney.
Woodfull is struck on the back as he ducks into a rising ball from Larwood.
The ball may be seen bouncing off him.

McCabe doubles up after being hit by Larwood in the shoulder.
Incidents such as these made Larwood a villain in the eyes of many Australians.
Larwood's Nottinghamshire captain, Arthur Carr,
wrote that Larwood had told him after his return to England that in Australia
'he had been spat at by larrikins in the crowd,
booed out of cinemas, and had to have police protection when he came out of hotels'.

In the fifth Test Larwood almost crowned his great success
with the ball throughout the series by scoring a century.
Sent in at number 4 (he normally batted at number 9 or lower),
he hit out lustily and raced to 98, only to be caught
by one of the poorest fieldsmen in the game, Bert Ironmonger.
He is shown here swinging the ball to the on boundary
to bring his score up to 50.

Oldfield runs out Ames for 4 in the fifth Test after taking a smart return from Bradman.
The decision was considered at the time to be a dubious one,
and this picture lends weight to the view that Ames may have been unlucky.
(A Fishwick Photo)

Jardine caught by Richardson off the bowling of
Ironmonger for 24 in the fifth Test.

Bradman gets Allen away for runs behind square leg in the second innings of the fifth Test. Woodfull is the other batsman. Note the packed offside field to which Allen was bowling — a conspicuous contrast to the legside fields set for the other fast bowlers. This innings by Bradman, his last against a bodyline attack, was probably the most spirited he played that summer against the English bowlers. Pelham Warner later wrote: 'Bradman was in his most dominating mood and made the most amazing strokes off Larwood and Voce, stepping away from his wicket and forcing the ball from the off. His first four was a sort of smash which you see at lawn tennis.' *The Sydney Morning Herald* said: 'Bradman caused the crowd to gasp at times when he drew away to the legside to attempt to force the ball through the covers.' In fact, he was so successful at hitting Larwood to the vacant offside field that two men from the bodyline trap were moved to square on the offside. He reached 50 in seventy minutes, and at last it looked as if he had the bodyline bowlers at his mercy. Jardine was clearly worried, for he changed his field repeatedly. Then the unexpected. In trying to drive Verity, Bradman hit over a well-pitched ball and was bowled. He had made 71.

Wyatt edges a ball to McCabe in the fifth Test.
The other Australians, from left,
are Richardson, Oldfield and the Victorian left-handed batsman L. P. O'Brien,
who played in two of the Tests.

For more than 40 years this was described in various cricket books as a picture of Don Bradman carrying the drinks in the second Test of the 1928–29 series. The assumption was made because that was the only first-class match in which Bradman was twelfth man. In fact, the picture was taken on the last day of the fifth Test of the bodyline series. Bradman carried the drinks because he had been hit high on the left arm by Larwood on the previous day and the arm was still too sore to allow him to field. This picture appeared in *The Sydney Morning Herald* on the following day. The blow to Bradman's arm in the fifth Test was the only one he sustained in the eight matches he played against the Englishmen that summer, which is itself a tribute to the swiftness of his feet. This is the account Jardine gave of how Bradman was injured: 'Bradman was hit only once, when struck on the arm with a ball from six to nine inches outside the leg stump which he was attempting to cut.'

Hammond hits the Australian off-spinner P. K. Lee
for six to bring up the winning runs in the fifth Test
and so bring the series to an end.
Oldfield is behind the stumps and McCabe is the fieldsman.
(A Fishwick Photo)

Hammond and Wyatt, who is carrying a stump as a souvenir,
leave the field after scoring the winning runs in the last Test at Sydney.
Hammond was 75 not out and Wyatt 61.
Thus ended the most controversial of all cricket series.
There were no official speeches to mark the occasion,
but Woodfull did visit the English dressing room to congratulate Jardine.
In the Australian dressing room, Vic Richardson got the team together and gave
Woodfull three rousing cheers.
In the newspaper next day, the Australians' final declaration of support
for their captain was described as 'touching'.

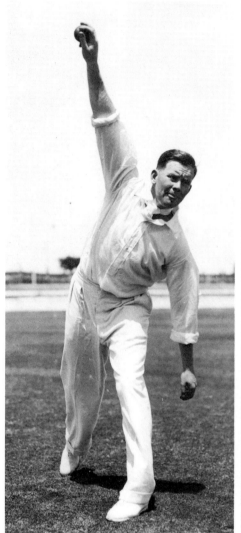  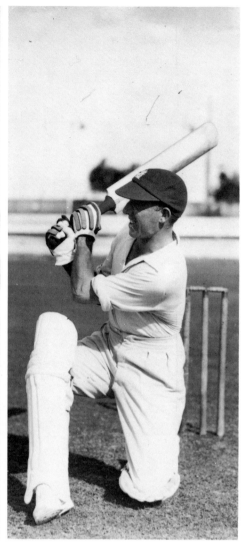

1

Freddie Brown was the youngest and one of the least conspicuous members of the English team. Omitted from all the Tests, he scored only 186 runs on the tour and took 18 wickets. Brown was the longest survivor of Jardine's party. He captained the English team that toured Australia in 1950–51 and was more successful with both the bat and ball than he had been 18 years before. He still wore the same kind of neckwear then that he is seen wearing here in 1932–33.

2

'I thought I had better hit Verity before Larwood hit me,' Bradman is reported to have said in explanation of the urgency with which he attacked Verity's bowling. The cricket writer R. W. E. Wilmot expressed it this way: 'He [Bradman] felt in himself that he must take the gifts the Gods offered while he had the chance.' The above picture of Verity was taken during the tour.

3

Eddie Paynter in 1932–33. Although he ended up heading the batting averages in the Tests on both sides, Paynter had not been chosen in the original touring party. He was brought in as a replacement for Duleepsinhji, who had to pull out of the team.

4

Les Ames admits today that he had misgivings about the fairness of bodyline during the tour. 'Behind the scenes, perhaps, I didn't approve of it,' he says. Out of loyalty to Jardine, however, he avoided discussing the ethics of bodyline with any other player.

5

Stan McCabe. 'He is in the line of Trumper,' Neville Cardus said of him, 'and no other batsman today but McCabe has inherited Trumper's sword and cloak.'

6

It is necessary to speak to some of the Englishmen who played against Stan McCabe (above) to appreciate how much his batting was admired. He was considered by them to not just another great batsman, but to be a batsmen of absolutely exceptional class. Gubby Allen, for instance, believes McCabe's performances in Test cricket, fine though they were, never did his ability full credit. Allen believes McCabe would have been a much more successful batsmen if there had been no Don Bradman. The presence of such a prodigious scorer higher up the batting order weakened his incentive to score runs himself.

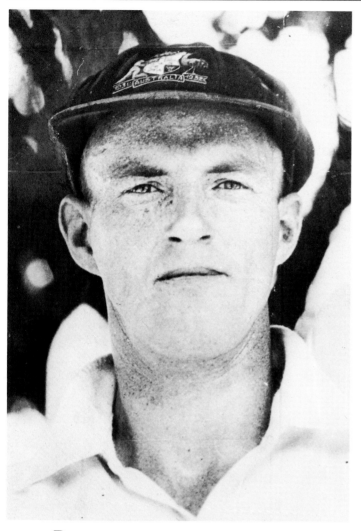

Bill O'Reilly was Australia's most successful bowler by far during the bodyline series, taking 27 wickets at an average of 26·8. It was during this series that O'Reilly established himself beyond doubt as Australia's best bowler, a reputation he was to retain for the rest of the 1930s.

That bodyline was effective is clear from the fact that it reduced Bradman's average in the Tests to 55·6, about half of what it probably would have been otherwise. However, the performance of other Australian batsmen suffered even more than Bradman's. Bill Ponsford (above), the opening batsman, was one of these. Before the bodyline series he had been one of the heaviest scorers in the game's history, once holding the world record in first-class cricket, 437. (This record was taken from him by Bradman.) In the three Tests he played in 1932–33, however, his scores were: 32, 2, 85, 3, 19, 0. His average was thus 23·5. Ponsford and Bradman obtained revenge of a kind 18 months later when, in the fifth Test of the 1934 series against England, they made a world-record partnership of 451, Ponsford scoring 266 and Bradman 244.

This is Bill Bowes's assessment of Jardine (above) more than 50 years after he played under him: 'He was one of the greatest men that I've ever met. He was a great friend, but a very fierce enemy. He didn't expect anything and he didn't give anything. This went through his whole life. He had single purpose, but he could be changed by argument. He didn't like argument — he liked his own way. If I had a criticism of him at all — this is as far as cricket is concerned — it was that he expected the less able perhaps than himself to do things of which they were not capable.'

Bradman's methods of trying to counter bodyline was then, and has been since, a subject of controversy. When criticized about them, Bradman was able to answer that they were more successful for him than other tactics were for all the other batsmen. This is how R. W. E. Wilmot, a journalist who covered the series, described Bradman's methods: 'He ducked and ran. With more imagination than the others, he decided to stand well back from the wicket. Instead of the centre-and-leg guard he had previously adopted, he took block on the leg stump. He endeavoured by hitting the ball on the offside to force Larwood to weaken his leg field, and it was marvellous to watch some of his strokes. They were his own invention. They brought him many runs, but they also cost him his wicket. The fight between him and Larwood went on match after match, and in the third Test at Adelaide he was again the master, only to lose his wicket to the slow bowler, Verity, as a result of over-confidence.' Jardine was one person who disagreed with Bradman's tactics. Referring to Bradman's century in the second Test, Jardine later wrote: 'He adopted more orthodox methods. Why he ever deserted such methods will always remain a mystery to me, for, relying on them on this occasion, he obtained the complete mastery which so many Australians associate with his batting.'

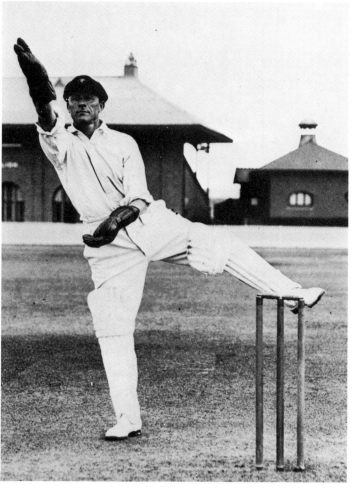

Bill Bowes (posing awkwardly, above, during the 1932–33 tour) tells of a potentially nasty incident which occurred when he, Larwood, Voce and Leyland were drinking in a bar at Brisbane. 'A bushwhacker, I think he was, came in and said, "What's this bodyline?" Larwood said, "Don't talk about that — cricket's over for the day. Come and have a drink with us." This fella says, "I want to talk about it," and he slams a revolver on the counter and says, "This'll probably make you." So Harold Larwood says to Bill Voce, "Bill, come and stand here." So Bill Voce moved over and he says, "Hey, put that in your pocket." This fella turned round to argue with him, and Bill Voce hit him. What happened then I don't know, because the bar emptied like a flash.'

Having stood down with some reluctance from the fourth Test because of the skull fracture he suffered in the third, Oldfield was back behind the stumps for the fifth. Carrying on from where he left off at Adelaide (he was on 41 there when he had to retire hurt), Oldfield made 52 in the first innings of the fifth Test and finished the series with a Test average of 27·2. This was higher than the averages of Fingleton and Ponsford and only a fraction below Richardson's.

Wally Hammond, above. Regarded as the premier batsman in Jardine's team. He had a fine season in the Tests, scoring two centuries, an 85 and a 75 not out. In spite of this, his average for the series, 55.0, was still lower than Bradman's, 56.6 — and Bradman was reckoned to have failed!

With hair neatly in place as always, Herbert Sutcliffe, above right, practises a drive for the camera. Sutcliffe and Hammond were the most successful English batsmen in the Tests, each scoring the same number of runs, 440, for the same average, 55.0. However, Sutcliffe was easily the most successful in all first-class matches, heading both the aggregates (with 1,318) and the averages (73.22).

The English spinner Tommy Mitchell. He played in only one Test (the fourth), taking three wickets. He also had a hand in dismissing Bradman in that Test when the Australian was looking highly dangerous. Bradman had been using his now-familiar tactics against Larwood's bodyline — stepping back to slam the ball to the off — and in one over he had scored 12 runs, twice cutting Larwood off successive balls to the boundary. Jardine moved Mitchell to point to block this shot, and in Larwood's next over Bradman hit a catch straight to him.

Bill Woodfull was considered in some Australian quarters to be too mild a character to be an effective counter to Jardine, but it seems none of his players agreed with this. Bill O'Reilly says: 'I completely and utterly respected him. When he said something, he meant it. There was sufficient about him for any man to respect.'

A mainstay of England's bowling attack throughout the 1930s, Hedley Verity was one of Britain's saddest casualties of World War II. He was wounded in Sicily and later died in an Italian prisoner-of-war camp in 1943.

For most of 1933, the Australian tour of England scheduled for the following year seemed in danger of being cancelled because of the MCC's unwillingness to guarantee that bodyline would not be bowled by the English team. The MCC balked at giving such an undertaking, for to do so would have been to admit that bodyline was unfair, which it was not yet ready to concede. Cables went back and forth between England and Australia, but by December 1933, the matter had still not been settled. In the meantime, Aubrey Oxlade (left) had become chairman of the Board. Oxlade, a leading New South Wales cricket official, believed the cancellation of the 1934 tour should be avoided at all costs. He said so in a letter to the then chairman of the Board, Dr Robertson, on 20 June 1933. After the became chairman, Oxlade held out for a no-bodyline assurance from the MCC, but when by 12 December the MCC still refused to give it and seemed reconciled to the tour being cancelled, Oxlade capitulated. On 14 December he drafted a cable confirming that the tour would go ahead and told the Board's secretary, Jeanes, that he would send it 'immediately I get a majority of Board members in favour'. Once again the Board had given in to the MCC. Less than three weeks later, when the New Years honours were announced, Oxlade was named as the recipient of a CBE. This gesture from London was probably intended to reward Oxlade for being so conciliatory as well as to soothe Australian feelings. Punch magazine joked that Oxlade might have been given the Order of the Garter if one had been found big enough to fit leg-theory.

Don Bradman, above. His comparative failure against Jardine's men did not seem to affect his tremendous standing with the Australian public. This is probably because most Australians believed he had been deprived of success by unfair means. It must also be recognized that Bradman's failures in 1932–33 were confined to matches against the Englishmen. In Sheffield Shield matches that season he scored 600 runs in five innings for an average of 150·0.

Jack Fingleton, above right, was later to succeed with his typewriter where he had failed with his bat. In the mid-1940s he wrote a book about the bodyline series called *Cricket Crisis,* which most critics would consider one of the finest cricket books ever written. Almost certainly, it is the finest cricket book written by an Australian — and this does no injustice to Ray Robinson. Fingleton seems to have been inspired when he wrote it, which probably indicates the emotional impact that bodyline made on him.

Bill Voce, right, holds a pose for the camera in 1932–33. Voce was coach of Nottinghamshire when the Australians touring under Don Bradman played the county in 1948. Perhaps remembering how Australians had suffered at the hands of Nottinghamshire pace men, Ray Lindwall bowled with special purpose that day, taking 6 for 14. It was said to have been the fastest he had bowled at that stage of the tour.

After their return to England, Jardine presents Voce and Larwood
with security certificates worth £388 each.
The money had been collected by Nottingham newspapers.

The West Indian all-rounder Learie Constantine, pictured here at Sydney in
January 1931. Partnered by another fast bowler, E. A. Martindale, Constantine
bowled bodyline in a Test against the Englishmen in 1933, only a few months
after their return from Australia. Hammond had his chin badly gashed by a
bouncer and is reported to have said that he would quit the game if such tactics
were persisted with. Four Englishmen — Hammond, Wyatt, Ames and C. F.
Walters — fell victim to bodyline, but Jardine stood up to it and made 127.
Australians were inclined to make little of his performance, however, claiming
that neither Constantine nor Martindale could bowl bodyline so fast or so
accurately as Larwood. However, the West Indians' bodyline attack made such an
impression on the editor of Wisden, Sydney Southerton, that, while accepting it
was only a "pale imitation" of Larwood in Australia, he was still prepared to say:
"What they did was sufficient to convince many people with open minds on the
subject that it was a noxious form of attack not to be encouraged in any way."

Jardine, a proud father, photographed at Loch Rannoch,
Scotland in September 1935.
There is no doubt Jardine mellowed as he grew older.
The renowned Australian cricketer Keith Miller
met him after the war and found him extremely pleasant.
'We had dinner with him at Oxford,' Miller says.
'He was the most polite man you'd ever meet — a marvellous host.
I thought what a nice old guy.'
Jardine did have one peculiarity of behaviour, however.
An old business associate in London says he used to buy small numbers of shares,
perhaps as few as 10, in a lot of companies
and then attend their annual meetings.
This photograph was kindly provided by Jardine's daughter,
Mrs Fianach Lawry.

After his term as Governor of South Australia, Sir Alexander Hore-Ruthven
was for a short time Governor of New South Wales and then,
from 1936 to 1944, Governor-General of Australia.
As Lord Gowrie, he became president of the MCC in 1948.
He appears to have been instrumental in securing a knighthood
for Don Bradman in the following year.
Among papers presented to the National Library in Canberra by Lord Gowrie's family,
there is a letter written to him by Lord Nuffield on 27 May 1948,
in which the knighthood is suggested. Lord Nuffield wrote:
'I venture to put to you the following suggestions which I am sure
would do much to cement the good feeling
that exists between the Commonwealth of Australia and Great Britain.
Don Bradman, who is now in this country and will be playing in the last Test match,
can rightly be termed the king of cricketers of this age and is,
I feel, entitled to some form of recognition, preferably a knighthood.'
We know Lord Gowrie acted on the suggestion,
for among his papers there is also a letter to him from Buckingham Palace,
dated 1 June 1948, in which the suggestion is discussed.

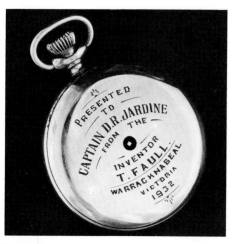

This ball-counter was one of the souvenirs
of the 1932–33 tour which Jardine kept for the rest of his life.
It is now in the possession of his daughter, Mrs Lawry.

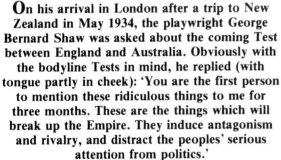

On his arrival in London after a trip to New Zealand in May 1934, the playwright George Bernard Shaw was asked about the coming Test between England and Australia. Obviously with the bodyline Tests in mind, he replied (with tongue partly in cheek): 'You are the first person to mention these ridiculous things to me for three months. These are the things which will break up the Empire. They induce antagonism and rivalry, and distract the peoples' serious attention from politics.'

The Board's chairman during the series, Dr Robertson, was ready to take a hard line against the MCC. After the Board had sent its first, provocative cable to the MCC, Dr Robertson told the Board's secretary, Jeanes, in a letter: 'My own personal feeling in the matter is that I would go so far as to cancel the next Test games and all the Test games for the next 10 or 12 years, but of course I am only one of the number.' Later that year Robertson's term as chairman expired and he was replaced by Oxlade. In December, when Oxlade prepared a cable to the MCC agreeing to the 1934 tour without the MCC's assurance that bodyline would not be used, Dr Robertson was incensed. On 15 December he said in a letter to Jeanes: 'The precipitant action of the chairman renders my reply futile and superfluous except that it will record my disapproval. Firstly, no team should be sent until a definite promise was received that the methods objected to [bodyline] would be barred.' Dr Robertson said Oxlade had 'exceeded his powers'.

When the Englishmen next came to Australia, in 1936–37, they found Bradman a much more formidable opponent. In the last three Tests of the series he made scores of 270, 212 and 169. This picture shows him in a Test at Melbourne that summer pulling a no-ball from Gubby Allen straight back over the bowler's head, watched by three other veterans of Jardine's team — Ames behind the stumps, Hammond at gully, and Verity at point.

Robert Menzies, as Australian Prime Minister, and Douglas Jardine, during the latter's visit to Australia in the early 1950s. Jardine's daughter, Mrs Lawry, says the two men became good friends. In his book *Cricket Between Two Wars,* Pelham Warner makes an interesting reference to Menzies, who at the time of the bodyline series was Victorian Attorney-General. After discussing the Board of Control's cables to the MCC, Warner wrote: 'Subsequently these cables were toned down, and I often wonder whether Mr Menzies had anything to do with this.' There does not seem to be any evidence that he did, although Warner's reference certainly suggests that he may have. It would not be too surprising if Menzies did speak to the Board's chairman, Dr Robertson, or even to the Prime Minister, Mr Lyons. All three were in Melbourne at the time.

Harold Larwood emigrated to Australia in 1950, partly at the instigation of Jack Fingleton. Fingleton arranged hotel accommodation for the Larwoods when they arrived in Sydney, and, unbeknown to anyone but Fingleton, the Australian Prime Minister, Ben Chifley, paid half the bill. Larwood, who had by this time taken to wearing glasses regularly, is shown here with two veterans of the bodyline series, Bert Oldfield (left) and Clarrie Grimmett. Larwood and Oldfield became good friends.

The Nawab of Pataudi on the Orontes, October 1932. Pataudi is said to have been deeply hurt by abuse he received from the Australian crowds. He was called, variously, Potato, Pat O'Dea and Gunga Din, and had questions shouted at him such as 'Where's your loin cloth?' and 'Where's your goat?'

H. W. Hodgetts, of Adelaide, one of the four Board of Control members who drafted the first, controversial cable to the MCC. Hodgetts is probably best remembered in cricket history as the man who lured Don Bradman to South Australia. Late in 1933 Hodgetts offered Bradman a job in his stockbroking firm which, after due consideration, Bradman decided to accept. It was a decision which cost Bradman's home State, New South Wales, dearly.

Jack Fingleton the journalist. After newspapers published the story of how Warner was rebuked by Woodfull in the dressing room, Fingleton was blamed for leaking it to the journalists. In his book *Cricket Between Two Wars,* Warner said 'a member of the Australian XI who was connected with the Press' was responsible, which effectively pointed the finger at Fingleton, for he was the only professional journalist in the team. For as long as he lived, Fingleton denied the allegation. He claimed it was Bradman who leaked the story, and said he had been told this by Claude Corbett, the Sydney *Sun* journalist, who actually passed on the story to the other journalists at Adelaide. Bradman, for his part, has denied the allegation as emphatically as Fingleton. As recently as 1983, Mike Coward of *The Age* quoted Sir Donald as saying in an interview: 'It is a complete and utter fabrication. I did not leak the story to the press and I think Fingleton only made that charge against me to shift the feeling against him. I never heard the remark in the dressing room and I never leaked the story. It has always been my belief that Fingleton was the culprit.' Sir Donald went on to tell Coward that he was particularly incensed by the fact that Fingleton did not cite Corbett as a witness in the affair until after Corbett was dead. The whole question is a curious one, not least because leaking the story was not really so reprehensible in the first place. If the story had not been leaked, cricket literature would be much the poorer for it.

The great English batsman Herbert Sutcliffe. The Australian players considered him to be one of the strongest supporters of bodyline in the English team. Bill O'Reilly recalls: 'We used to regard him as an ex officio captain. Sometimes he would initiate the bodyline field.' Asked to explain this, one of Sutcliffe's team-mates in 1932–33 said recently: 'Well, he was a Yorkshireman.'

Bill Woodfull was a schoolteacher, and in his later years became principal of Melbourne High School. He died on 11 August 1965, shortly before his 68th birthday.

Ponsford in his later years. Ponsford was another Australian batsman who believed bodyline could not be mastered. He says today: 'I still don't think anybody in the world could have dealt with it.'

One of the last photographs of the two old adversaries, Harold Larwood and Bert Oldfield, taken together. It was taken at Sydney Airport in 1975 just before the two left for Hong Kong to attend ceremonies marking the closure of the old Hong Kong Cricket Club. Oldfield died the following year.

Harold Larwood, Sir Donald Bradman and Bill
Voce at the Centenary Test in Melbourne in
1977.

FIRST TEST

AUSTRALIA

W. M. Woodfull	c Ames b Voce	7	b Larwood	0
W. H. Ponsford	b Larwood	32	b Voce	2
J. H. Fingleton	c Allen b Larwood	26	c Voce b Larwood	40
A. F. Kippax	lbw b Larwood	8	b Larwood	19
S. J. McCabe	not out	187	lbw b Hammond	32
V. Y. Richardson	c Hammond b Voce	49	c Voce b Hammond	0
W. A. Oldfield	c Ames b Larwood	4	c Leyland b Larwood	1
C. V. Grimmett	c Ames b Voce	19	c Allen b Larwood	5
L. E. Nagel	b Larwood	0	not out	1
W. J. O'Reilly	b Voce	4	b Voce	7
T. W. Wall	c Allen b Hammond	4	c Ames b Allen	20
	Sundries	20	Sundries	17
Total		360		164

	O	M	R	W	O	M	R	W
Larwood	31	5	96	5	18	4	28	5
Voce	29	4	110	4	17·3	5	54	2
Allen	15	1	65	0	9	5	13	1
Hammond	14·2	0	34	1	15	6	37	2
Verity	13	4	35	0	4	1	15	0

ENGLAND

H. Sutcliffe	lbw b Wall	194	not out	1
R. E. S. Wyatt	lbw b Grimmett	38	not out	0
W. R. Hammond	c Grimmett b Nagel	112		
Nawab of Pataudi	b Nagel	102		
M. Leyland	c Oldfield b Wall	0		
D. R. Jardine	c Oldfield b McCabe	27		
H. Verity	lbw b Wall	2		
G. O. Allen	c & b O'Reilly	19		
L. E. G. Ames	c McCabe b O'Reilly	0		
H. Larwood	lbw b O'Reilly	0		
W. Voce	not out	0		
	Sundries	30		
Total		524	(0 wkts)	1

	O	M	R	W	O	M	R	W
Wall	38	4	104	3				
Nagel	43·4	9	110	2				
O'Reilly	67	32	117	3				
Grimmett	64	22	118	1				
McCabe	15	2	42	1	0·1	0	1	0

England won by ten wickets

1932–33 TEST SERIES

SECOND TEST

AUSTRALIA

J. H. Fingleton	b Allen	83	c Ames b Allen	1
W. M. Woodfull	b Allen	10	c Allen b Larwood	26
L. P. O'Brien	run out	10	b Larwood	11
D. G. Bradman	b Bowes	0	not out	103
S. J. McCabe	c Jardine b Voce	32	b Allen	0
V. Y. Richardson	c Hammond b Voce	34	lbw b Hammond	32
W. A. Oldfield	not out	27	b Voce	6
C. V. Grimmett	c Sutcliffe b Voce	2	b Voce	0
T. W. Wall	run out	1	lbw b Hammond	3
W. J. O'Reilly	b Larwood	15	c Ames b Hammond	0
H. Ironmonger	b Larwood	4	run out	0
	Sundries	10	Sundries	9
Total		228		191

	O	M	R	W	O	M	R	W
Larwood	20·3	2	52	2	15	2	50	2
Voce	20	3	54	3	15	2	47	2
Allen	17	3	41	2	12	1	44	2
Hammond	10	3	21	0	10·5	2	21	3
Bowes	19	2	50	1	4	0	20	0

ENGLAND

H. Sutcliffe	c Richardson b Wall	52	b O'Reilly	33
R. E. S. Wyatt	lbw b O'Reilly	13	lbw b O'Reilly	25
W. R. Hammond	b Wall	8	c O'Brien b O'Reilly	23
Nawab of Pataudi	b O'Reilly	15	c Fingleton b Ironmonger	5
M. Leyland	b O'Reilly	22	b Wall	19
D. R. Jardine	c Oldfield b Wall	1	c McCabe b Ironmonger	0
L. E. G. Ames	b Wall	4	c Fingleton b O'Reilly	2
G. O. Allen	c Richardson b O'Reilly	30	st Oldfield b Ironmonger	23
H. Larwood	b O'Reilly	9	c Wall b Ironmonger	4
W. Voce	c McCabe b Grimmett	6	c O'Brien b O'Reilly	0
W. E. Bowes	not out	4	not out	0
	Sundries	5	Sundries	5
Total		169		139

	O	M	R	W	O	M	R	W
Wall	21	4	52	4	8	2	23	1
O'Reilly	34·3	17	63	5	24	5	66	5
Grimmett	16	4	21	1	4	0	19	0
Ironmonger	14	4	28	0	19·1	8	26	4

Australia won by 111 runs

THIRD TEST

ENGLAND

H. Sutcliffe	c Wall b O'Reilly	9	c sub. b Wall	7
D. R. Jardine	b Wall	3	lbw b Ironmonger	56
W. R. Hammond	c Oldfield b Wall	2	b Bradman	85
L. E. G. Ames	b Ironmonger	3	b O'Reilly	69
M. Leyland	b O'Reilly	83	c Wall b Ironmonger	42
R. E. S. Wyatt	c Richardson b Grimmett	78	c Wall b O'Reilly	49
E. Paynter	c Fingleton b Wall	77	not out	1
G. O. Allen	lbw b Grimmett	15	lbw b Grimmett	15
H. Verity	c Richardson b Wall	45	lbw b O'Reilly	40
W. Voce	b Wall	8	b O'Reilly	8
H. Larwood	not out	3	c Bradman b Ironmonger .	8
	Sundries	15	Sundries	32
Total		341		412

	O	M	R	W	O	M	R	W
Wall	34 1	10	72	5	29	6	75	1
O'Reilly	50	19	82	2	50·3	21	79	4
Ironmonger	20	6	50	1	57	21	87	3
Grimmett	28	6	94	2	35	9	74	1
McCabe	14	3	28	0	16	0	42	0
Bradman					4	0	23	1

AUSTRALIA

J. H. Fingleton	c Ames b Allen	0	b Larwood	0
W. M. Woodfull	b Allen	22	not out	73
D. G. Bradman	c Allen b Larwood	8	c & b Verity	66
S. J. McCabe	c Jardine b Larwood	8	c Leyland b Allen	7
W. H. Ponsford	b Voce	85	c Jardine b Larwood	3
V. Y. Richardson	b Allen	28	c Allen b Larwood	21
W. A. Oldfield	retired hurt	41	absent hurt	0
C. V. Grimmett	c Voce b Allen	10	b Allen	6
T. W. Wall	b Hammond	6	b Allen	0
W. J. O'Reilly	b Larwood	0	b Larwood	5
H. Ironmonger	not out	0	b Allen	0
	Sundries	14	Sundries	12
Total		222		193

	O	M	R	W	O	M	R	W
Larwood	25	6	55	3	19	3	71	4
Allen	23	4	71	4	17·2	5	50	4
Hammond	17·4	4	30	1	9	3	27	0
Voce	14	5	21	1	4	1	7	0
Verity	16	7	31	0	20	12	26	1

England won by 338 runs

FOURTH TEST

AUSTRALIA

V. Y. Richardson	st Ames b Hammond	83	c Jardine b Verity	32
W. M. Woodfull	b Mitchell	67	c Hammond b Mitchell ..	19
D. G. Bradman	b Larwood	76	c Mitchell b Larwood	24
S. J. McCabe	c Jardine b Allen	20	b Verity	22
W. H. Ponsford	b Larwood	19	c Larwood b Allen	0
L. S. Darling	c Ames b Allen	17	run out	39
E. H. Bromley	c Verity b Larwood	26	c Hammond b Allen	7
H. S. Love	lbw b Mitchell	5	lbw b Larwood	3
T. W. Wall	not out	6	c Jardine b Allen	2
W. J. O'Reilly	b Hammond b Larwood .	6	b Larwood	4
H. Ironmonger	st Ames b Hammond	8	not out	0
	Sundries	7	Sundries	23
Total		340		175

	O	M	R	W	O	M	R	W
Larwood	31	7	101	4	17·3	3	49	3
Allen	24	4	83	2	17	3	44	3
Hammond	23	5	61	2	10	4	18	0
Mitchell	16	5	49	2	5	0	11	1
Verity	27	12	39	0	19	6	30	2

ENGLAND

D. R. Jardine	c Love b O'Reilly	46	lbw b Ironmonger	24
H. Sutcliffe	lbw b O'Reilly	86	c Darling b Wall	2
W. R. Hammond	b McCabe	20	c Bromley b Ironmonger ..	14
R. E. S. Wyatt	c Love b Ironmonger	12		
M. Leyland	c Bradman b O'Reilly	12	c McCabe b O'Reilly	86
L. E. G. Ames	c Darling b Ironmonger ..	17	not out	14
G. O. Allen	c Love b Wall	13		
E. Paynter	c Richardson b Ironmonger	83	not out	14
H. Larwood	b McCabe	23		
H. Verity	not out	23		
T. B. Mitchell	lbw b O'Reilly	0		
	Sundries	21	Sundries	8
Total		356	(4 wkts)	162

	O	M	R	W	O	M	R	W
Wall	33	6	66	1	7	1	17	1
O'Reilly	67·4	27	120	4	30	11	65	1
Ironmonger	43	19	69	3	35	13	47	2
McCabe	23	7	40	2	7·4	2	25	0
Bromley	10	4	19	0				
Bradman	7	1	17	0				
Darling	2	0	4	0				

England won by 6 wickets

FIFTH TEST

AUSTRALIA

V. Y. Richardson	c Jardine b Larwood	0	c Allen b Larwood	0
W. M. Woodfull	b Larwood	14	b Allen	67
D. G. Bradman	b Larwood	48	b Verity	71
L. P. O'Brien	c Larwood b Voce	61	c Verity b Voce	5
S. J. McCabe	c Hammond b Verity	73	c Jardine b Voce	4
L. S. Darling	b Verity	85	c Wyatt b Verity	7
W. A. Oldfield	run out	52	c Wyatt b Verity	5
P. K. Lee	c Jardine b Verity	42	b Allen	15
W. J. O'Reilly	b Allen	19	b Verity	1
H. H. Alexander	not out	17	lbw b Verity	0
H. Ironmonger	b Larwood	1	not out	0
	Sundries	23	Sundries	7
Total		435		182

	O	M	R	W	O	M	R	W
Larwood	32	10	98	4	11	0	44	1
Voce	24	4	80	1	10	0	34	2
Allen	25	1	128	1	11·4	2	54	2
Verity	17	3	62	3	19	9	33	5
Wyatt	2	0	12	0				

ENGLAND

D. R. Jardine	c Oldfield b O'Reilly	18	c Richardson b Ironmonger	24
H. Sutcliffe	c Richardson b O'Reilly ..	56		
W. R. Hammond	lbw b Lee	101	not out	75
H. Larwood	c Ironmonger b Lee	98		
M. Leyland	run out	42	b Ironmonger	0
R. E. S. Wyatt	c Ironmonger b O'Reilly .	51	not out	61
L. E. G. Ames	run out	4		
E. Paynter	b Lee	9		
G. O. Allen	c Bradman b Lee	48		
H. Verity	c Oldfield b Alexander ...	4		
W. Voce	not out	7		
	Sundries	16	Sundries	8
Total		454	(2 wkts)	168

	O	M	R	W	O	M	R	W
Alexander	35	1	129	1	11	2	25	0
McCabe	12	1	27	0	5	2	10	0
O'Reilly	45	7	100	3	15	5	32	0
Ironmonger	31	13	64	0	26	12	34	2
Lee	40·2	11	111	4	12·2	3	52	0
Darling	7	5	3	0	2	0	7	0
Bradman	1	0	4	0				

England won by 8 wickets

Australia Batting Averages in the Test Matches

	M	I	R	HS	NO	Average
D. G. Bradman	4	8	396	103*	1	56·57
S. J. McCabe	5	10	385	187*	1	42·77
L. S. Darling	2	4	148	85	0	37·00
W. M. Woodfull	5	10	305	73*	1	33·88
P. K. Lee	1	2	57	42	0	28·50
V. Y. Richardson	5	10	279	83	0	27·90
W. A. Oldfield	4	7	136	52	2	27·20
J. H. Fingleton	3	6	150	83	0	25·00
W. H. Ponsford	3	6	141	85	0	23·50
L. P. O'Brien	2	4	87	61	0	21·75
L. E. Nagel	1	2	21	21*	1	21·00
H. H. Alexander	1	2	17	17*	1	17·00
E. H. Bromley	1	2	33	26	0	16·50
A. F. Kippax	1	2	27	19	0	13·50
C. V. Grimmett	3	6	42	19	0	7·00
W. J. O'Reilly	5	10	61	19	0	6·10
T. W. Wall	4	8	42	20	1	6·00
H. S. Love	1	2	8	5	0	4·00
H. Ironmonger	4	8	13	8	3	2·60

*not out

Australian Bowling Averages in the Test Matches

	I	O	M	R	W	Average
T. W. Wall	7	160·1	33	409	16	25·56
W. J. O'Reilly	9	383·4	144	724	27	26·81
H. Ironmonger	8	245·1	96	405	15	27·00
P. K. Lee	2	52·4	14	163	4	40·75
D. G. Bradman	3	12	1	44	1	44·00
L. E. Nagel	1	43·4	9	110	2	55·00
C. V. Grimmett	5	147	41	326	5	65·20
S. J. McCabe	8	92·5	17	215	3	71·66
H. H. Alexander	2	46	2	154	1	154·00
A. F. Kippax	1	2	1	3	0	—
L. S. Darling	3	11	5	14	0	—
E. H. Bromley	1	10	4	19	0	—

England Batting Averages in the Tests against Australia

	M	I	R	HS	NO	Average
E. Paynter	3	5	184	83	2	61·33
W. R. Hammond	5	9	440	112	1	55·00
H. Sutcliffe	5	9	440	194	1	55·00
R. E. S. Wyatt	5	9	327	78	2	46·71
Nawab of Pataudi	2	3	122	102	0	40·66
M. Leyland	5	9	306	86	0	34·00
H. Verity	4	5	114	45	1	28·50
H. Larwood	5	7	145	98	1	24·16
G. O. Allen	5	7	163	48	0	23·28
D. R. Jardine	5	9	199	56	0	22·11
L. E. G. Ames	5	8	113	69	1	16·14
W. Voce	4	6	29	8	2	7·25

Also batted: W. E. Bowes 4* and 0*. T. B. Mitchell 0.

*not out.

England Bowling Averages in the Tests against Australia

	I	O	M	R	W	Average
H. Larwood	10	220	42	644	33	19·51
T. B. Mitchell	2	21	5	60	3	20·00
H. Verity	8	135	54	271	11	24·63
W. Voce	8	133·3	23	407	15	27·13
G. O. Allen	10	170·6	29	593	21	28·23
W. R. Hammond	10	120·3	27	291	9	32·33
W. E. Bowes	2	23	2	70	1	70·00
R. E. S. Wyatt	1	2	0	12	0	—

Bibliography

The Larwood Story (Bonpara, 1982) by Harold Larwood
with Kevin Perkins

Cricket Crisis (Cassell, 1946) by J.H. Fingleton

Bodyline Umpire (Rigby, 1974) by R.S. Whitington and
George Hele

Bradman and the Bodyline Series (Angus & Robertson) by
E.W. Docker

The Cricket Captains of England (Cassell, 1979) by Alan
Gibson

Follow On (Collins, 1977) by E.W. Swanton

Cricket With the Lid Off (Hutchinson) by A.W. Carr

Three Straight Sticks (Stanley Paul, 1951) by R.E.S. Wyatt

Farewell To Cricket (Hodder & Stoughton, 1950) by Sir
Donald Bradman

Cardus On Cricket (Souvenir Press, 1949) by Neville Cardus

Sir Donald Bradman — A Biography (B.T. Batsford, 1978)
by Irving Rosenwater

Cricket Between Two Wars (Sporting Handbooks, 1942) by
Sir Pelham Warner

Defending The Ashes, 1932–33 (Robertson & Mullens) by
R.W.E. Wilmot

The Book of Cricket (J.M. Dent, 1934) by Pelham Warner

In Quest of the Ashes (Hutchinson) by Douglas Jardine

Observer article, November 7, 1982, by Peter Deeley

Ashes — and Dust (Hutchinson) by Douglas Jardine

Don Bradman's Book (Hutchinson) by Don Bradman